Late For My Plane

Confessions of an Ordinary Mystic

By

Michelle Senjem
and
Rebecca LeTourneau

Cover Art by Mike East and Rebecca LeTourneau

ISBN: 0-7596-7061-7

This book is printed on acid free paper.

1stBooks – rev. 04/17/02

We would like to thank the following people for their poetry contributions:

Mike East
Mark East
Christina LeTourneau

Questions or comments about this
book should be directed to

Mystic Waves, Inc.
PO Box 756
Forest Lake, MN 55025

Michelle Senjem
continues to give readings by appointment.
For more information, email: mijanjyl@msn.com

or visit the Mystic Waves website at
www.mysticwaves.com

This book is dedicated to:
Vivian Nordin Harris
who created a life worth living from the abyss of hell
and made us laugh about it all.

and to:
John Alfred East
whose direction and support from the other side
brought this work into being

Acknowledgments

From Michelle:

This book was born from the courage and inspiration of many human travelers. I would like to say thank you to a few of these magical friends without whom this story would not exist.

To my husband Bruce who is always strong by my side and who makes me believe he is absolutely the kindest man on the planet.

To my son Christopher for being my metaphysical guide and study partner and a world of inspiration. Because of his amazing vision and honesty I find it easy to believe in miracles. To my daughter Jillian for teaching me more about who I am than anyone else on earth. She has always been a straightforward guide to the truth for me and her shining spirit is a most remarkable gift to my life.

To all my siblings who lived this story with me: Richard, Gary, Marlene, Pam, Michael, Mark and Terry. Each one of you remains a constant source of support and love. To my mother Vivian whose courage and humor ultimately set us all free to find a life worth living. To my father, John who coached me through the writing of this book from the other side where he lives more fully and lovingly than he could here.

To Rebecca for finding me so that we might express our passions more joyfully than we ever could have without each other and for the way you listen and hold my hand. To the following people who continuously steer me back to myself: LeAnn, Jana, David, Patty, Carol, Louise, Blanche, Dawn, Linda, Nancy, Sheila and Wendy. Thank you for enriching my life.

From Rebecca:

This project could not have been completed without the support, love and inspiration I received from the following gems in my life: To my husband Larry whose constant support and faith has sustained me through the years. His stubborn belief in my work has often surpassed my own, for which I am forever grateful.

To my children, Larry III and Christina, I thank you for your inspiration and love that seems to follow me everywhere. I have learned more from being your mother than I have from anything or anyone else in this world. To Mary Masi for applauding every new endeavor I become a part of, including this remarkable story. You inspire me to the stars every time. To Ed and Ruth Andrews for their constant love and support even when they think I'm over the edge...

To Patricia McSorley for challenging me to higher levels and for always believing this story should be told. To Michael East whose generosity and visions of beauty overwhelm me. To Michelle for trusting me with your words and vision. Your way of seeing the world is a gift from beyond and one I will forever treasure. To Baji for his subtle influences, which continually amazed me while at the keyboard - his presence could not be missed.

There is a small bird
aloft in flight,
higher than most,
flying as the wind
decides.

Introduction
by Michelle Senjem

    I have been strongly connected to my Spirit Entity all my life but didn't begin to realize it until my early twenties. By 'Spirit Entity' I mean a group of beings who are connected to a particular human, kind of like an 'oversoul' group. We are each a part of a Spirit Circle, being the flesh and bone manifestation for the Group during this physical lifetime, and throughout our earthly experiences we are accompanied by the rest of the Group whether we realize it or not. The most comforting aspect for me in knowing this fact lies in the understanding that I am not alone - not ever. None of us are. Although we may sometimes feel as though there is nothing connecting us to the Divine, this is merely an illusion for we are all connected *all* the time and will be for eternity. Awareness of this connection is an entirely different matter, however!

    Those in my Spirit Circle reveal themselves to me periodically in many different ways and through a variety of means. I am not certain exactly how many there are but at times I suspect that my Spirit Circle overlaps with those of others who in turn overlap with others still... and on and on until all are connected, all are a part of each other. But for now, for the purpose of this physical lifetime, I need only be concerned with those in my immediate circle because they are the ones who assist and comfort me. They are the ones guiding my steps, helping me to trudge through dilemmas and sidestep disasters, tossing thoughts into my head, whispering timely reminders into my ears and pointing out the questions I need to be asking myself.

    My interesting spirit-friends have provided me with many adventures, both of the mind and of physical reality. They beckon to me with visions and dreams and with glimpses of the future or the past. They tantalize my imagination with endless possibilities. Often, they reach out to me through humorous antics and ridiculous poses, reminding me not to take myself or them too seriously. Yet, at other moments, they move forward to embrace me with a flowing, swirling love and support, encouraging me to go on, to move forward through nightmarish pain and crippling anxiety.

Out of the many beings I have come to know and treasure in my Spirit Circle, one has emerged as my most central guide and closest confidant. The fact that he revealed himself to me as a kind of magical character in children's storybooks served to remind me of his presence in my life as a young girl, when I would communicate with him so naturally I didn't even realize the significance of it. His appearance is a constant source of comfort to me even though I know it is merely an illusion created for the benefit of my human experience, presented to me as a visual gift so that my conscious mind has an image it can grasp and hold onto even during my weakest moments.

I have come to understand that all of those in my Spirit Circle are me; they are various parts of myself, but this is not to say they are mere projections of my unconscious mind. The truth is much simpler than that. Being human we see ourselves only in the limited form of the physical individual without realizing there are many other dimensions to one's soul. These other dimensions include the presence of other beings who are separate from us in one sense yet are a part of the whole of who we are. Without them I am not complete; without me they are not complete either. I have been told that many twins and triplets and other multiple birth partners are participating in an earthly adventure where two or more of one's Spirit Circle agree for whatever reasons to enter into the earth realm together. So, although they are separate physical beings and may have vastly different interests, they are a part of the same Spirit Circle, each of them contributing to the good of the whole in their own way.

It is also possible, sometimes, that two or more within a particular Spirit Circle will manifest themselves in human form at the same time yet may never even meet one another while in the earth realm. Even then, however, each member of the Circle is contributing to the whole and both are assisting one another during their physical lifetimes without being consciously aware of it.

I have been blessed in my experiences and adventures here on the earth planet, surprising myself many times and providing much entertainment to those of my Spirit Circle. They often tease me about the ease with which I become distracted and my tendency to drift here and there, always eager to sample the many different delights of this physical existence. Always, they are patient with me. Even during the times when I have ventured down unsteady and destructive paths, ignoring their warnings and insistent calls, they have never wavered in their utter love for me.

Throughout the many adventures and experiences recorded in this book, I was receiving information and gentle guidance from those in my spiritual family, much of which I have included in each chapter. The messages I received, and continue to receive from them, move me to share what they tell me with others - since this seems to be in alignment with my purpose for being here in this body at this time. This brings me joy. Knowing this, my Spirit Guides often lead me to ask some very profound questions, which they eagerly address as if they have waited for centuries to do just this.

Most of what I have presented here was channeled through me by the one guide who is most constantly available, as I mentioned above, the one who seems almost a spokesman for the Group at times. He can be tricky, shifting into female form when it is more convenient to speak from a female perspective, then back into male form again - sometimes right in front of my eyes! Every once in awhile, he will even speak to me in both voices simultaneously as if to remind me that the sexes are not so different after all - at least not at the spiritual level.

As a male, he calls himself Baji, and as a female he is Mija. I cannot explain how I know that Baji and Mija are one and the same being - I just *do*. The others I have met in the Group are very distinctly male or female but are not as prevalent or as constant in my conscious life. They will appear periodically when it is meaningful for them to do so and then will fade back into the spirit realm, ever near but silent unless I specifically seek them out. I know that I have had my turn in their place many times as one or another of them participated in human form, taking on the role of a physical lifetime themselves. Right now it is my turn to take on this role. It isn't my first time doing this but it is the first time I have been manifested in *this* body, the first time I have chosen to look at the world through the eyes of a woman named Michelle Senjem, the first time I have taken part in this *particular* adventure.

It seems we have decided, in our Spirit Group, that Baji/Mija would be my closest assistant this time around. It is a role he/she relishes, I can tell you. It is an endless source of comfort and encouragement to me, knowing that this special spirit friend is such a willing participant in my day-to-day activities. Without him/her, and without the others in my Circle of Being, I would likely be floundering somewhere on a slippery road, arms outstretched, my hands groping desperately through the dark, searching for something to hold onto.

She fades back into my dream mind
Tomorrow if I feel unsettled again
I will find her waiting.

Baji and The Little Princess

In a white turban and purple silk clothing, Baji seemed to float next to me, his bronze skin glowing. I felt his dark eyes resting on me as I waited, trying to be patient.

"You are excited," he said. It was merely an observation, not a judgment, and I did not deny it.

"She seems to be in so much pain," I told him. He nodded, turning his gaze back to the writhing woman on the hospital bed below us. We had been watching her for hours now, as she twisted and moaned in agony. She did not know we were aware of her, carefully observing her every move, listening to her every gasp of despair. This woman, who was to be my birth mother for an entire physical lifetime, had no idea I was preparing to embark upon another journey into the earth realm. Long ago, I chose her to be my birth parent and she agreed, but now I could not remember the reasons for my choice. I recognized the familiar feeling of my spirit-memory slipping away from me as the time for my physical birth drew near.

Vivian, the woman on the bed, had been in labor for many tortured hours. Surely, it would be time for me to go soon! I was anxious to get started, my emotions already shifting toward those associated with basic comforts such as infants are concerned with. A thrilled anticipation filled my senses along with vague recollections of warm arms and breasts, soothing tones, and heavenly maternal comfort. I didn't think I could wait much longer; my earthly future was beckoning!

But, Baji seemed to be holding me back. Something in his manner and in the aura surrounding his quiet form caused me to hesitate.

"What is it?" I asked, impatiently.

"Listen."

I listened closely to Vivian's groans as they grew more and more desperate. She was beginning to thrash back and forth with

1

increasing fervor until a stern-looking nurse moved forward to hold her down.

"Hush," the nurse told her, "don't carry on like that. It's just a baby, not the end of the world."

She spoke briskly, her face impassive as she looked down at Vivian's flushed cheeks. I did not like her tone of voice or her harsh manner either. She stood over the bed like some kind of angry military officer, a disapproving frown clouding her narrowed eyes as my mother recoiled from her touch.

"Women have been having babies for thousands of years," the nurse barked, tightening her grip on Vivian's arm.

"She needs comfort, not a lecture," I told Baji, indignantly. Already, my loyalties were drawn toward this tormented woman below me. I could feel our earthly connection beginning. My observation of her was no longer one of simple interest and compassionate fascination; now I was filled with a tension deep within my being. It actually hurt to watch her suffer so. I felt anger toward the insensitive nurse whom Baji seemed to be defending.

"She thinks she *is* being a comfort," he said, "it's the best she knows how to do."

"Well, it's obviously not enough. Look, look, my mother is crying!"

Indeed she was, as her struggle against the nurse's restraint gave way to muffled sobs. Then, another pain seized her and the agonized moaning started again. Oh, this was too much! Surely, I had not come to the brink of birth only to watch my chosen earth mother die while trying to bring me into the world!

"I have to go," I said, desperately, "this is lasting far too long, Baji. It's too much for her."

"Yet, we must wait," he replied, quietly. He urged me through his silent gaze to calm myself. I tried to do as he asked but my heart was yearning to comfort my future mother. If I were to just go ahead and enter that tiny body and emerge into

2

the physical world I could end her suffering and provide the relief she so badly needed.

"Is that what you think?" Baji asked, gently.

"I ... I think so, yes."

He smiled a patient, rather sad little smile and spoke to me in his usual loving way.

"You have already begun your journey, I see. You have forgotten where we came from and what this is all about. This is good because it shows your willingness to go where you have planned to go and to learn those things you have so long desired to learn. But, right now, I want you to try and calm yourself. Try to slow your thought process way, way down and just let yourself feel what she is feeling."

It was difficult to follow these directions but I struggled to do as he asked, and after a bit I was able to tear my attention away from a sobbing Vivian long enough to focus on Baji's face. As I did this, a feeling of peace and utter love swept through me, enabling me to disconnect from my anxiety. Through the strengthening energy of my compassionate friend I was able to gather up the patience needed to look at my mother in a more objective way. I concentrated on her feelings - on her deep heartfelt emotions.

"Can you feel what she is feeling?" Baji asked.

"Yes, she is in terrible pain."

"But what is going on beneath her present reality? What is lurking in the shadows of her unconscious? Go deeper than the obvious."

Surprised that I might be missing something, I focused my energy intently, allowing myself to feel Vivian's spirit as well as her deepest agony. I did not hold back but let my vision penetrate through walls of shame and sorrow until the full force of her desperation stormed through me. I gasped at the intensity of her nightmarish memories. Labor pains were not the sole cause of her anguish. Actually, they had nothing at all to do with her tormented spirit. Rather, she was seized by a terror so powerful and all consuming it was nearly choking her to death.

The sorrow that filled her was so vast it encompassed the pain of women from all over the world. From centuries past and present, faceless, raging women who were victims of abuse, neglect, humiliation, and loss had embedded their collective misery and despair within every beat of Vivian's heart. So much suffering attached to one's gender! I cringed from the perspective I was descending into, viewing the world from the windows of my mother's eyes. So many heartaches endured simply because one was born female, experienced only because of the way the world seemed to work in favor of men, even the ones who were bitter and angry and violent.

Vivian did not understand the unfairness of it; she could not get her mind around it. I could sense her utter confusion and her rage. Her opinion did not matter because she was a woman. She had no value, no worth whatsoever because she was female. Even her body was not her own; men had abused it, abused it, abused it - because of her gender.

"She thinks this world is a terrible place for women," I whispered to Baji, "she does not want this baby to be a girl."

"This is her reality," he replied, softly.

"It's so... so *strong* in her," I said, sadly.

"Yes."

Baji and I watched Vivian for a bit longer, absorbing the magnitude of her pain and examining its implications within our own spirits. How strong one's perceptions of reality could be! How profoundly people were shaped by their experiences! I was amazed by how fiercely Vivian clung to her way of seeing the world.

Finally, Baji turned to me, his dark eyes filled with compassion.

"Not yet," he said, "not this time."

"No?"

I wasn't sure I understood him at first, but already I was being pulled back into the shimmering world of the Spirit Womb, back to Safety and Perfect Love. Baji was still beside me, murmuring gentle reminders about the eternal nature of time and about the complete and total healing that visits every soul eventually. I felt a familiar acceptance and contentment enter my being as I floated effortlessly alongside my tender friend. The anxieties and indignation I felt while watching Vivian drifted easily away from me as I realized my earthly adventures would have to wait. For some reason it was necessary that I experience this near-birth. I knew without a doubt that I would understand it all eventually, and a serene peace filled me as I embraced this truth.

As I was slowly following Baji back into the Light and the Wonder, Vivian's cries grew more and more faint behind us. Her writhing subsided at long last, giving way to an immense relief when the doctor announced in a grave voice that the baby girl was stillborn. Already dead when she came out. Already back in the realms of Forever where I would remain for yet another year.

The memory of this pre-birth experience did not come back to me until, as an adult, I had a very vivid and mind-shattering dream. In this dream I revisited the events and circumstances surrounding my birth in perfect detail, complete with every emotion, every thought, every worry, every feeling. When I awoke from this ordeal I was in a state of shock, for I remembered each and every bit of the dream experience as if I had actually lived it the day before! I sat there in my bed unable to move or speak as I moved through the experience again in my mind.

It dawned on me then that I had always been attracted to the storybook image of the Indian magician in purple silk clothing and a white turban. Now, I felt sure I knew why. Perhaps this Baji-spirit, who was obviously connected to me in a very powerful way, had chosen this image to present to me during the moments just before my birth so that I would be left with a lingering memory of his appearance. This affection for such Baji-type images, even during my earliest childhood days, provided me with many moments of comfort during times when I was sad or troubled. I would sit by myself daydreaming about a mystical Indian fellow who soared above the earth on a magic carpet, taking my worries with him to some distant shore. Even today, my husband works for a company called ALADDIN!

After dreaming so clearly about Baji and my physical birth, I became much more aware of his presence in my life. I had seen other visions and other spirit forms but I had never seen this particular one - this Baji - before. Why was he so elusive to me? I determined to pay close attention to what was happening around me on a daily basis, feeling that maybe I was overlooking something.

When I told some of my family and friends about my amazing dream, most of them were skeptical. It was just a dream, they said. Probably just a product of my overactive imagination. All my life I have heard people talk in this dismissive way about dreams but even as a young girl I knew that dreams will connect us to our spiritual roots. Too many times dreams have opened very real doors for me in my life and I know better than to be so flippant about them. But, how could I possibly explain the intensity of my feelings during and after this particular dream experience? I couldn't really blame those who thought the whole thing was mere fantasy because I knew how incredible it sounded. But I could not deny the truth of it, myself. I could not forget the way it felt, the way it seemed so very *real*.

Some time later, a woman performed a reading for me. I didn't know her, but I'd read about her in a local new-age newspaper. We spoke briefly before our session, exchanging pleasantries about the weather and recent events in the news, getting to know one another a little bit so the hour would be comfortable. However, I immediately sensed her to be kind and honest so was eager to get started.

"I don't really have any major questions," I told her, "but I have been experiencing some blockage lately when I try to tune into my spirit guides."

I wanted her to focus on my energy field and see if maybe she could pick up on something I might be missing.

"Oh, I have those times, too," she replied, sympathetically. I liked her open nature and had no trouble relaxing in her presence. It was a relief to find someone who practiced psychic work who was comfortable with her flaws. I have met some wonderful psychic-oriented people in my life but have also met quite a few who are incredibly arrogant and critical of others. Just like many experts in other fields, some psychics feel the need to come across as infallible. This woman, whom I will call Shannon, had no ego problems whatsoever, as far as I could tell.

As we sat there quietly facing one another, Shannon suddenly mentioned in an off-handed manner that there was a nice-looking man in a white turban looking over my shoulder.

"He looks like Ali Baba," she said, and laughed.

"I know him!" I exclaimed.

"Do you?" she asked, squinting toward the air behind me.

"Yes, yes," I said, excitedly, and proceeded to tell her about my dream. She seemed neither impressed nor skeptical, but appeared to just take it in stride.

"I'm not getting any communication from him," she said, "he is just kind of *there*."

Immediately, I realized that indeed, he had always been 'just kind of there' around me, watching, comforting, and gently guiding me at different times while never making himself too visible or distracting.

After Shannon saw Baji hovering over my shoulder, however, he began to reveal himself to me more and more. He continued to visit me in my dreams periodically but would also appear in the form of a purple energy mass while I was awake, projecting his soft voice into my head. Other times, I would feel his presence around me in a most intense fashion but would see and hear nothing from him, only receiving messages in thought form, deep inside. With time, he began to enter into my physical being so that he could speak through me, using my voice, which led me to share his insights with others more and more often.

Whatever form he uses to communicate, I know he is ever near, just a thought away at any given moment. Always a comfort, he leads me to the hidden truths within myself time and again.

Going back in time with Baji to the moments just before my birth into this world served to heal a great many wounds I had harbored deep within - wounds of which I hadn't even been aware. I understood for the first time the state of mind and being my mother was in when she gave birth to me, and so was filled with a new compassion and love for her. Seeing things from a higher, more overall perspective like that can change a person at a very deep level and in a most profound and everlasting way. Long-held beliefs and shadowy uncertainties are wiped away as new clarity takes root. Nothing heals so completely as this.

I was able to tell my mother that the baby girl who was born dead so long ago was not some mysterious lost soul - she was me! I was able to describe the way it felt - to almost go through with it only to be turned back toward the Light at the last instant. I explained to her that this experience was in alignment with a Greater Good, and that someday she would understand and be grateful for it. There was no reason for her to harbor feelings of guilt because of her emotional state at the time for this, too, has been a valuable lesson on many levels and to many souls and spirits.

For some reason, I was not meant to enter into physical life at that time; both my mother and I were to experience that birth-death situation instead. However, the following year she and I were to meet again under very similar circumstances. Only, this time I was encouraged to go forth and enter into my earth life without further delay.

When it came time for my second encounter with Vivian, which was also revealed to me during that initial, awe-inspiring dream, I was not so eager to enter into earthly existence. Just twelve months had passed; did my future mother feel any differently now than she had the last time? I hesitated next to Baji who held a calm silence as I sought out Vivian's emotional state once again.

It was immediately apparent to me that her opinions had not changed. She was still filled with dread at the very idea of bringing another female child into the world. In her mind the two daughters she already had were two too many - just two more who would experience the abuse and neglect and utter helplessness Vivian associated with their gender. This was the truth my earth mother had come to believe so deeply as she moaned in agony once more.

No, I did not want to go there. I did not wish to enter into Vivian's world of misery and sadness, especially when I could still feel the warmth and safety of the place I had come from! But Baji was encouraging me to go. He urged me gently forward, forward...

"But wait," I said, hesitating, "I'm not sure I'm ready, Baji..."

However, his reassuring smile calmed my fears. He reminded me of the courage in my nature and about how so many others in the spirit realm were also looking forward to my upcoming earth experience with great interest. He expressed heartfelt appreciation for my willingness to partake in this adventure and said that it was not only for the sake of my own spiritual expansion but for the benefit of others as well.

I began to relax as I listened to Baji's soft voice in my ear. Something in those wise, dark eyes told me it was going to be all right. He would be with me; we were going to embark upon this earthly adventure together.

"I know you don't remember right now," he said, kindly, "but we have been through this before."

I trusted him. I knew at that moment that I had always trusted him, this gentle loving friend, and that he would never fail me. An overwhelming sense of love and peace flooded through me, giving me the courage I needed. I gazed upon Baji's face, feeling his utter devotion to me.

It was time.

So, with Baji's love surrounding me, I let myself go. I allowed my being to disconnect from that brilliant world of Light long enough to fall freely and willingly on the wings of Trust into the body of a screaming female infant, much to poor Vivian's disappointment.

Four years later I was jumping up and down with excitement, tugging on my mother's arm.

"Is it for me, Mommy, is it for me?"

"Well, hmm..." my mother said. She smiled down at me. "Maybe we should ask Daddy."

She winked at my father who sat in his favorite chair across the room pretending to read the newspaper.

"Daddy, Daddy!"

I raced over to scramble up his leg until I was perched in place of the paper that had crumpled against his chest. He heaved a loud, exaggerated sigh and looked at me, his blue eyes twinkling.

"Now, now, what's all this about?"

"Mommy has a box, look! A box from the departer store —"

"Department," Mommy broke in, sounding shocked. "Department store, dear."

"The depart-ment store, Daddy, is it for me?"

"Well," Daddy said, rubbing his chin thoughtfully, "you know, I think ... ah..."

I clasped my hands together beneath my chin and held my breath.

"...umm ...you know..." he said, "...I think it *is* for you, Michelle!"

I let out a gleeful screech and bounded to the floor again, heading for that box so fast my feet barely touched the carpet. Mommy laughed.

"Easy now," she said. But I had already ripped the top off the lovely cardboard box and was staring open-mouthed at what lay inside.

"Oh," I gasped.

"Hold it up, sweetie," Daddy said.

With great care, I lifted the beautiful red dress out of the box and held it up under my chin.

"Oh, it's a princess dress isn't it Mommy? A real live princess dress?"

"Well, you are a little princess, aren't you?" Mommy asked, blinking hard. Daddy cleared his throat and rattled his newspaper.

"Sure is pretty sweetheart," he said, "but you had better put it up now, before it gets dirty."

"Oh, can't I put it on, please, please?" I begged.

Mommy smiled patiently and held out her hand. "Not just yet, little one," she said, "but you come and help me find a safe place to hang it, okay? It's for a special day next week. You can wear it then."

"A special day, really?"

I took my mother's hand as we walked upstairs to the bedroom. I clutched the dress to my chest being careful not to drag it on the floor.

"Yes," Mommy told me, "we are going to court next week. People always dress up when they go to court. It's a very important day, Michelle. Your brothers and sisters will be there, too."

"Oh, they will?"

I was happy to hear this. I liked to play with my brothers and sisters. They lived far away in a house somewhere in the city but came to visit sometimes. There were so many of them! Five boys and two girls, all of them bigger than me except for Baby Terry

11

who couldn't even talk very well yet. My brothers and sisters called me "Baby" sometimes, too, but not in a bad way. They teased and tickled me, making me laugh, and they had lots of stories to tell. Because they went to school already, they knew about the world of teachers, recess, and lunch boxes and I never tired of hearing about these unfamiliar things.

Sometimes, the boys would fight with one another, shouting and pushing, rolling around on the ground and calling each other bad names. But I was not afraid of them because they had never hurt me. Also, they could run, jump, and climb better than any boys I had ever seen. Mike and Mark would play war, whooping and dodging as they shot imaginary bullets at one another. Tor and Gary would pick me up, swinging me around by my arms as I laughed and laughed, and Marlene and Pam would share their dolls with me every time they came over. It was nice to have so many brothers and sisters. I couldn't wait for them to see me in that magnificent new dress! I hoped Mommy would take a picture of me in it. She could hang it on the wall in the living room with the other one. The one that was up there now had been taken when I was just a baby and I didn't like it - my cheeks had been so fat!

The next few days seemed to drag on forever. I kept running to the closet in Mommy's room to gaze adoringly at the dazzling red dress where it hung so stiff and proper on that padded hanger. Oh, I wanted to wear it!

Mommy tried to help me keep my mind off it, doing lots of things with me so the time would go faster. We played games, read stories together, and she took me to the park a few blocks away. I loved going to the park with Mommy. There were always other children there to play with. Some of them could only stay a short while before their mothers would whisk them away but my mother let me stay as long as I wanted. And Daddy helped to keep me busy, too. He bought me ice cream and gave me horsy rides on his back.

"Hah!" I would cry, slapping his back and he would snort and buck until I screamed with laughter, hanging onto his shirt for dear life.

Still, I couldn't stop thinking about the dress. When no one was looking I would slip upstairs and into Mommy's closet to touch it, letting the silky cloth slide through my fingers. I imagined myself walking through a flower garden wearing this magnificent garment, a fairy wand in my hand.

Finally, it was the night before we were to go to court and I sat on Mommy and Daddy's bed, barely able to contain my excitement. Mommy was twisting my wispy blond hair into curlers so I would have princess hair in the morning.

"Is court far away?" I asked, trying hard to sit still.

"Not so far," Mommy answered, quietly. She snapped the last curler into place and turned me around to face her.

"Do you remember your other Mommy and Daddy?" she asked.

"Oh, yes," I said, nodding happily. I liked the way the curlers felt bouncing against my head.

"Do you remember what me and Daddy told you about them, about how your brothers and sisters all live with them now?"

"Uh-huh. My brothers and sisters live with my other Mommy and Daddy in the city, right?"

"That's right. And... well, they... your other Mommy and Daddy are going to be at court tomorrow, too."

"Oh, is it going to be a party?"

My eyes lit up. That other Mommy and Daddy, the ones who were called Birth Parents, seemed nice enough. They would come into the house once in a while when they came to pick up my brothers and sisters. They never said too much, though.

"Well, not exactly," Mommy said. She sighed and gazed tenderly at me for a moment. Then, she reached out to pull me into a close, warm hug.

"Is it going to be like a princess party, maybe?" I asked, my cheek crushed against my mother's cotton housedress.

"Not really, dear. But you will certainly look like a princess, that much I know!"

I giggled. I wrapped small arms around my mother's neck and squeezed tightly.

"Thank you," I said, dreamily, "thank you for my red dress."

"There, there."

Mommy pulled away and got quickly to her feet, dabbing at her eyes with a clump of Kleenex.

"Must be my allergies acting up again," she said, but I wasn't listening. I was already making a beeline to the closet so I could get one last glimpse of my beautiful new dress before going to bed.

The courthouse seemed like a palace to me and I imagined I was a princess as I swished along next to my mother in my red dress. The wide marble steps and high ceilings made me feel like I was walking into another world. All the woodwork around the massive doors was beautifully carved into intricate little flowers and leaves and the huge, long windows sparkled in the sunlight.

We stopped in front of a wide door with a brass handle and Mommy said I would have to wait out in the hall. She pointed to a long bench along the wall where my brothers and sisters sat, all in a row.

"Stay right here with them, okay dear? I won't be long."

"Okay."

I was proud to parade my dress back and forth in front of the others. I twirled and giggled and twirled some more, flipping my blond curls this way and that.

"Better sit down," Pam told me. Pam was older and knew so many things, I felt compelled to obey her. I sat, but couldn't keep from bouncing up and down on the bench. I leaned into my sister Marlene, then into Pam, then into Marlene again...

"Hey," Marlene said, "sit still, why don't you?"

Tor, our oldest brother, leaned forward to look down the row at me.

14

"Don't you know you're in a courthouse?" he asked, frowning.

"Huh-uh, I'm in a palace," I replied, happily, "and I'm a princess and you're a... a ...a sort-man."

"A what?" Gary asked. He leaned forward, too.

"A sort-man. And so are you..." I pointed to each one of my brothers in turn, "and you, and you."

"What's a sort-man?" Mark wanted to know.

"You ride a horsy," I explained, "and you have a mask on and you have a sort and you hit the bad guy off his horsy. You hit all the bad guys, all the bad guys!"

I leapt from the bench, brandishing one arm, swatting it back and forth over my head.

"Hah! You see? You hit them all off with your sort."

"She means sword," Pam said, a half-grin on her face. "She is calling you guys swordsmen."

The boys chuckled and laughed.

"Sort-men," Mark said, nudging Gary.

"I'm gonna kill you with my sort," Gary told him, grinning.

"Yeah," I shouted, jumping up and down, "kill him with your sort!"

"Ssh," Pam said, looking around.

"God, you're loud," Tor said. He groaned and slapped his palm into his forehead.

I bounced on tiptoe, holding out the edges of my skirt so I could curtsy. Yes, yes, thank you, thank you, I am a movie star princess, thank you very much...

"Come on," Pam said, patting the seat beside her, "you have to sit down before we get into trouble."

I giggled. I hopped back up between my two sisters and tried to sit still but it was hard. I wanted to dance and sing, laugh and twirl; I was a princess today! What was wrong with everybody?

Mommy was no fun, either. She emerged from behind that wide door, her face strained and pale, and told me in a small, curt voice that it was time to go home.

"Oh, but my picture," I protested, pulling on her hand.

"What?"

"My picture. You said you would take a picture of me in my new dress."

"Oh," Mommy said. She put a hand to her eyes, "I'm sorry, I forgot my camera, Michelle. We'll take one when we get home."

"But I want to play with them," I said, pointing to the bench where my brothers and sisters sat, still-faced, watching us.

"Later, dear. You'll have plenty of time for that..."

Mommy's voice broke and I looked up in surprise to see a tear slipping down her cheek.

"What's the matter?" I asked, bewildered.

"Nothing, dear," Mommy said, sniffling, "nothing at all. But we do have to go, okay?" She cleared her throat loudly, blinked her eyes hard and the tears were gone. I watched her, confused. Then, I turned to look back at that door Mommy had come through.

"What does that say?" I asked, tugging at my mother's hand, "wait, wait... what does that say?"

Mommy paused, sighing. "What does what say, dear?"

"That," I pointed to a long black plaque on the door.

"Oh. That says Judges Chambers." Mommy pulled on my hand. "Now, we really have to go."

I had no choice but to walk along beside my mother, down those wide marble steps, across that gleaming hall and out into the sunlight. I was so disappointed! I hadn't even had a chance to play with my brothers and sisters. It wasn't fair! I wanted to run down those echoing hallways in my hard dress shoes, slide down those smooth, winding banisters. Why did we have to go home so soon? But Mommy wasn't talking and when we got back home she went into the bathroom, shut the door and didn't come out for a very long time.

This was no fun. I went upstairs to my room and sat on my bed. Daddy should be home soon. Maybe he would give me a horsy ride on his back again. I looked down at my red dress. What a beautiful dress!

"I'm a princess," I whispered. Then, I started to chant louder and louder, "I'm a princess, I'm a princess, I'm a princess..."

I stood up on the bed and began to jump. Higher and higher off the bed I jumped, the ruffled red dress flouncing all around me. When Mommy came into the room a few moments later, I watched her warily, wondering if I would get into trouble for jumping on the bed in my hard shoes. But Mommy didn't seem to mind. She had a suitcase, which she opened up on the dresser top and began to pack my clothes into.

"Are we going somewhere?" I asked, still jumping.

"Just you, dear."

Mommy sounded stuffed up, like she had a cold.

"Where am I going, where am I going, where am I going?"

"To be with your brothers and sisters, Michelle. You'd like that, wouldn't you?"

"Yes, yes, yes," I shouted in a singsong voice, "I want to go and play, I want to play all day, all day, all day..."

"Well, now."

Daddy was in the doorway. I stopped jumping and looked at him guiltily. But he just smiled gently as he came in the room. I watched as he crossed the floor and put his arms around Mommy. They stood like that, with their arms around one another for a long time. Then Daddy turned and beckoned to me with his finger.

"Come on, sweetheart. We're going to take a little ride into the city, okay?"

"Okay."

I bounded off the bed and into my father's outstretched arms. Then, suddenly, my face was being squished between two warm hands and I realized with surprise that my mother was covering me with urgent kisses on my forehead, my cheeks, my nose. So many kisses! And then she was gone, vanished from the room like a ghost and I sat, somewhat befuddled, in my father's embrace. He carried the suitcase in his free hand as we walked slowly downstairs.

"Isn't Mommy coming with us?" I asked in a small voice.

"Oh, she isn't... she isn't really feeling very well," Daddy said. I grew quiet, settling back against his broad chest. It was nice to be carried. I was a big girl now, four years old, but it was still nice to be carried once in a while, I decided. Especially since no one was around to see.

But as we crossed the threshold at the front door and stepped out into the warm day, I heard a strange sound coming from behind me, an awful, wailing sound. I had never ever heard anything like it before. It was the sound of uncontrolled sobbing, of a heart being broken to bits, a dream being dashed to pieces. That horrible, piercing noise cut through me like a knife, shocking me into silence. For the first time in my life, I suspected that my world might not be so safe and comfortable as I had imagined.

Daddy placed me gently into the front seat beside him as he climbed in behind the wheel and I sat, unmoving, as he drove past the quiet suburbs and headed into the noisy, cluttered city. I sat in my new red dress, my legs crossed at the ankles princess-style, and sang a princess song to myself. I did not sing out loud this time, but under my breath where only me and Baji could hear.

Years later, after I was married and had two children of my own, I experienced something that would cause me to relive those days in my early life and, consequently, prepare me to meet up with Baji again. It was just a few months before I went through the amazing birth experience dream with him that I woke up one day with a horrible migraine. I had suffered from migraines before but this was the worst yet and it didn't go away. This one, which lasted for ten days, drove me to absolute desperation. Oh, the pain! I really didn't think I was going to survive it that time. Bruce, my husband, was driving a semi-truck somewhere in the vast regions of America so I called my friend Jana to come over and help out with my two young children since it was becoming impossible to get out of bed. She assisted me for that entire week, playing with Chris and Jill, fussing over me, cleaning my house, and reading the kids stories at bedtime. Day after day that unbearable pain dragged on, rendering me quite helpless. Nothing seemed to help. I cried, shoveling pain medication into my mouth as I cowered beneath the covers praying for relief.

On the tenth day of this insanity I was driven to take refuge in my son Chris' room. For some reason, I wanted to lie on his bed and look at all his toys and stuffed animals scattered about, feeling they brought me some small level of comfort. I lay there, paralyzed with pain, wondering how I was going to make it through the next hour, much less the rest of the day when suddenly, I began to hallucinate. The sky seemed to open up right there in the ceiling above me as brilliant colors swept through the room. The air around me became vibrant and alive with a shimmering, flowing energy. Oh no, I thought, I'm dying. This is what dying is like!

A sharp pain seared through my heart as all at once a vision of my foster mother, Joan, appeared before me. I stared at the image of her as she tried to keep me from seeing her tears while packing my clothes into a suitcase. My god, there she was! The memory of her enveloped me with such force I was unable to move. For two decades, I had kept thoughts of her buried somewhere deep inside, not wishing to be disloyal to my birth family, but now the grief I had experienced in the loss of my first mother washed over me with a vengeance and I wept for hours. Gulping with sobs, I rushed into the bathroom over and over again to be violently ill as all the years of suppressed memories and emotions came to light.

Jana held my head while I was sick, murmuring to me in soothing tones, telling me I was beautiful, I was loved, I was special and precious and a treasure to the world. Her maternal, nurturing nature vividly reinforced my memories of Joan until I could smell her perfume and hear her voice in my ear. Oh, how I had missed her! To be so loved by someone and then to be ripped away without warning from those loving arms, forever separated from the only mother I had ever known - the intensity of my loss filled me up, permeating my skin and bones, doubling me over with an agonized grief.

The extreme nature of this experience served to explode open a window in my psychic awareness that day, forever changing me. Through my gut-wrenching sobs and violent illness, I could feel my innocent self emerging again - that former, more trusting and happy self I had left behind with my first mother in that pleasant, cheerful home. I began to remember who I truly was - that small child who trusted her intuition, who had held an abundant faith in the goodness of life and the world.

My headache subsided as evening drew near and I was able to rest comfortably on my son's bed. It hit me then that he was four years old - the exact same age I was when Louis, my foster father, had driven me to the home of my birth parents and left me there. My beautiful little Chris was the same age right now that I had been when I was pulled away from a serene, carefree environment and thrust into the chaotic world of alcoholism and anger. How small I had been, and how vulnerable! I saw myself as a little girl, swept up in the torrential winds of change, fumbling for solid ground every which way I could think of, and I cried for her. I held her and soothed her and cried for her loss, her suffering and terror and loneliness.

Through the worst physical pain I have ever experienced (and I gave birth to two children!), I gained incredible new insights into my own true nature and was able to remember my authentic self, which I had long forgotten. I know now that this change in perspective is what allowed Baji to visit me again, entering my consciousness first through my dreams and later through visions and personal contact, revealing himself to me on many different levels and in various forms. I had to come to the point where my mind was open and my spirit was freed from that oppressive, heavy sadness and grief I had never expressed. Once these memories flooded back into me and I was able to acknowledge the loss I had always felt, my vision cleared and that unnamed fear lurking at the bottom of my soul vanished. This fear had been attached to the thought of knowing myself, which is always at the core of any spiritual exploration, and once I was shown some of the shadows of my being, I became strengthened by my own compassion and love for that little girl I had left behind so long ago.

Thus, I was in a place within my state of being that allowed Baji to come to me in my dreams, leading me by the hand back to a place I could not consciously remember, and through his loving guidance I returned to where it all started and was born again.

In remembering and reflecting on this experience, I received a visit from Baji. As always, his gentle guidance and insight helped me to sort out the meaning of it, leading me ever closer to understanding. As with many parts of this book, my spirit friends intervened to impart messages to me that are meant to be shared with others. Thus, I have included excerpts of Baji's sessions with me wherever they came up in connection with what I was writing about, as well as a few messages from others in my Spirit Circle.

Baji: *A cleansing is necessary for all who wish to be clearly intuitive. They need to undergo this cleansing process over and over again - sometimes to clear the way for new thoughts and creations or sometimes just to release outworn thoughts or emotions that are no longer needed.*

For some people, as with Michelle, it can sometimes be helpful to undergo the physical immobility illness demands, for this forces one to slow down long enough to become aware of what is truly going on inside and to face what needs to surface.

21

Everyone experiences loneliness and feelings of abandonment at some point while in the earth realm. At a very deep level, these emotions are the normal human response to feeling separated from the very secure and loving embrace of the Divine. What is helpful to remember is that this separation is an illusion that is temporary. Our spiritual roots are always with us; we are always connected even though we may not always know it. I include myself in this dilemma as well, for I have also been in human form many times so I recognize the anxious feelings of separation that seem to have no name or reason in the earthly sense. I know how confusing these feelings can be, but they are connected to the yearning humans have for what they have lost - the memory of who they are and of those they are so very connected to. This yearning, then, motivates action and serves as a driving force toward development so that everything continues to move forward as people make their way through the wondrous adventures of physical existence.

Michelle had come to a point in her self-exploration work where she was in need of a type of cleansing before she could advance further. Because her heart and mind were open, she was able to see the truth that had been hidden inside her for so many years. Still, it is a fearful thing, sometimes, for humans to allow Truth to surface, for with its re-emergence comes the realization of one's vulnerability. Trust in Spirit is essential. Michelle wanted to know herself, wanted to understand the true nature of her being, yet her fears caused her to become ill because she required this extra push in order to look where she dared not look. Physical pain can sometimes move people toward spiritual truths simply by the desperate nature of the predicament. This is not necessary for growth, but sometimes it is the chosen path because of hidden fears blocking the way.

Once a person experiences an awakening to hidden truths deep within the self it is often easier to return to this place again and again because the level of trust deepens as one realizes there is no reason to fear the truth. Although there will be times of hesitation and even dread, the memory of former breakthroughs will lessen the anxiety surrounding self-exploration. This was a breakthrough experience for Michelle, and even though she was to experience similar feelings in the future when certain truths were in need of being discovered, she did not choose to subject herself to the same level of physical pain in order to find it. This is because her level of trust had been strengthened by this initial experience and fueled her work thereafter.

*This is not to say that physical pain comes to people **only** because of a lack of trust, for there are many reasons for pain - as many as there are reasons for living in the human form at all. But a lack of trust is one way people can be led toward physical pain, especially if they are seeking out a truth they just can't seem to get at and are in need of a 'push'. The strengthening of trust in Spirit may not shield one from all further physical pain but it can alleviate the need for pain **as a vehicle toward understanding aspects of Self**. The understanding will come more easily, without need for drastic physical ailments if a person is deeply embedded in a trust of Spirit.*

The human body is a wonderful guide - it can tell you exactly what you need to know on many levels. If there is something wrong with the body, then there is something in your spirit that is trying to get your attention on a soul level. Pay attention! Your cells hold a memory of everything that has ever happened in your physical life. If something was especially confusing or painful, this memory will cling to and color every subsequent experience you have that falls into this physical or emotional area. If these memories are repressed or brushed aside, they can serve to alter your impressions of people, events, and even Self. This will often cause you to keep recreating similar events through unconscious efforts as the memories struggle to emerge toward release and understanding.

If these memories, or the ideas and thoughts they have created, remain stuck in the unconscious they will slow your energy down to a level that inhibits necessary chemicals in your body and this can have serious effects on the immune system. The balance of chemicals in your body is a wondrous and flowing miracle of physical life but can be seriously inhibited by truths that are not allowed to surface. The truth holds a force so powerful that it might kill you, literally, in order to be heard.

Be honest, always, when asking what it is you are feeling in your stomach, your head, your back, etc. Pay attention to any thoughts that surface, no matter how wayward they seem. Ask your body what it wants to express - you will be amazed by the conversations you can have with your toes, your legs or your neck! What age is that body part feeling? Who is it mad at? What is it afraid of? What does it need in order to improve its function and its support of the whole? Talk to your body, but even more importantly - LISTEN!

Transition wraps its dark claws around my heart
I run, frightened of its power
But it clings and I can't shake it

The terrain is changed.

The only way to bear it is to close my eyes
and I wonder if I am in the hell of death
or am I in the womb of life

Not yet born.

Michelle Senjem and Rebecca LeTourneau

Nightmares and Premonitions

My birth mother's head had been severed from her body and was rolling down the street toward me... oh no... no, I couldn't stand it, couldn't bear the image, the vision...

Horrified, I shook myself out of that awful scene. I turned in the darkness of my bedroom to call for her, terror gripping my stomach as I blinked to regain my senses - and there on top of the dresser beside me was her head! No body, just a head; oh my god, it was right there in front of me clear as anything, real as could be, lying sideways with those wide, dead eyes staring at me.

I screamed, leaping from my bed. Through the living room and the kitchen I ran as fast as I could until I reached my parents' bedroom. I stumbled through the darkness to their bed, my mind dizzy with shock.

"What is it, Michelle?"

Oh, that familiar voice; Vivian was alive, she was here in her bed next to my father John, her head still attached to her body! I jumped under the covers next to her, sobbing uncontrollably.

"Ssh, it's all right, honey," she murmured, still half asleep. A warm hand reached out to stroke my hair. "Tell me about it."

"I... I... you were dead... your head was on my dresser..."

Gulping with sobs, I managed to get the story out as Vivian listened sympathetically. She assured me it had only been a bad dream, it was okay now, there she was alive and well, right next to me.

"No," I said, earnestly, "it was real, it wasn't a dream. I woke up from my dream and *then* I saw it!"

"Oh, honey, of course it was a dream," Vivian said with a soft chuckle. "How could my head be on your dresser when it is sitting right here on top of my neck?"

Little by little she began to convince me that it had all been an illusion after all, that I had only dreamt waking up. My awful vision of her lifeless head began to subside a bit and I settled down at the foot of the bed, comforted by the warmth and nearness of my sleeping parents.

This pattern of sleeping with Vivian and John was becoming the norm for me. Just a few nights before I dreamed about a fanatic little boy who kept riding his tricycle back and forth next to my bed, refusing to let me sleep.

"Ha ha," he kept saying as his tiny eyes gleamed at me like two black dots in his pale, freckled face. He hadn't seemed like a dream to me either; he seemed real. I could feel the anger and the mean spirit in him; he didn't like me. He wasn't going to let me sleep no matter how tired I got. I tried to ignore him, tried to escape into a black, peaceful slumber but hadn't been able to get rid of him until I was safely tucked into the foot of my parents' bed again, sheltered from his cruel intentions by the steady rhythms of their breathing.

It seemed my dreams were always unsettling, always scary. I felt as though I were drifting off into a world where no one liked me, where people and animals and strange creatures wanted to terrify me. It was an unfriendly place, this world of dreams, and I did not want to go there anymore. I tried not to dream, prayed not to dream and fought the very idea of dreams with all my might and soul. But nothing was as horrible as the night Vivian's head appeared on my dresser. Nothing seized my heart with such a panic as that did; nothing bolted me from my bed and into my parents' bedroom so quickly.

The next day, I could still recall the terrible image of her head on my dresser but it was becoming easier to block it from my thoughts and after a few days I wasn't even thinking of it anymore. It joined the many other nightmarish images I had collected, cast away into some dark corner of my subconscious mind where I needn't be bothered with it anymore. Or so I believed.

About a week or so later, I came into the kitchen and found my mother weeping at the kitchen table.

"What's the matter?" I asked, alarmed.

"Come here," she said, wiping tears from her chin, "sit here, Michelle."

She patted the chair beside her and I sat, wondering what could have made her cry so hard. Was it something Daddy had done... something I had done?

"Tell me about your dream again, honey," she urged me.

"What dream?"

"The nightmare you had about me - about my head on your dresser."

Surprised, I sat back, trying to think. I didn't want to remember it but I would have done anything for her at that point, she was so upset. I went back into my memories, those awful horrid memories, and described them to her as best I could once again.

"It's just so strange," she said, when I had finished. "So very strange."

Then, she told me that one of her aunts had been driving in her car when a train hit her. Her head had been severed on impact and was sent rolling down the street!

Staring at her, round-eyed, I tried to absorb what she was telling me but all I could feel was relieved that it hadn't been my mother. It hadn't been Vivian. I didn't know this great-aunt of mine like my mother did so even though the whole thing sounded terrible, I didn't feel the grievous pain she was feeling at that moment.

"But why did I think it was you," I asked her, perplexed. "Why was it your head I saw?"

Vivian burst into tears again and handed me a crumpled photograph she had been holding. It was damp from her tears and a bit faded from age. I stared down at the woman in the photo, my great-aunt whom I had never met. It was incredible - I couldn't believe my eyes - she looked just like my mother! They could have been twins they looked so much alike. So, I hadn't seen my mother's head on the dresser, I had seen this woman's head and had assumed it was Vivian because it looked just like her!

When news of this event got out to the other family members, I was teased mercilessly. My brothers and sisters begged me not to dream about them, exaggerating their joking pleas in loud, high-pitched voices.

"I'm not going to die today, am I, Michelle?"

"God, don't think about *me* while you're falling asleep!"

"Dream about our gym teacher why don't you, maybe she'll have an accident before the mile run test next week."

I knew they were kidding, but there was also an element of fear behind their taunts, in me as well as in them. I didn't want to have any more dreams. I didn't want to know things before they happened - and what if I were causing awful things to happen by dreaming them in advance? This was a part of my life I could see no good in, and I tried and tried to deny and ignore it for many years to come.

Life with my birth family was very different from what I had been accustomed to and I often found myself completely bewildered by the change. I didn't understand these new rules where children were allowed to talk to one another in such anger and where the little considerations of my previous home seemed not to exist. The days did not follow any particular routine; everything just seemed to happen in a helter-skelter fashion until I wasn't sure of anything any more.

Also, we were poor. This was a new concept for me; I had never thought about money before or what the lack of it meant. Instead of having all the clothes and toys I wanted, I had to wait in line for the least little thing and even then I was lucky to get much of anything I wished for.

"I can't wear that dress to school," I told Vivian, "it's got a hole in it."

"Where?"

"Right there."

I pointed to the hemline where a small round hole suggested a cigarette had been near the garment in the past. Vivian chuckled.

"No one will see that," she said, waving a hand in the air. But I was sure the thing should be thrown into the trash.

My attitude and continual surprise at the lack of material comforts led to my being teased by my siblings who called me "Princess Michelle." This was no longer a fantasy label but a sarcastic, resentful one and I hated the very sound of the words.

"Look at her," they told each other, "she thinks she is so special."

"I do not," I protested, but I knew they were right. I *did* think I was special: Louis and Joan had always told me so. I was special, smart, pretty, funny, quick on my feet and I could sing and dance like a movie star. Only, it began to occur to me that not everyone thought so, which was an upsetting realization.

At first I cried a lot. I cried when I was allowed just two or three M&Ms out of the bag instead of getting the whole thing. I cried when I didn't get a turn on the rusted bike in the back yard and I cried when my brothers shoved me off the sofa so that I had to watch the rest of the television program from the floor. I cried when my sisters yanked me out of the way so they could use the bathroom first and I cried when the lot of them locked me in the basement, giggling on the other side of the door as I shrieked in panic because of all the monsters and spiders they had told me were down there. Of course, all this crying only led to more teasing.

"Baby Princess thinks she should get everything handed to her."

"Crybaby, crybaby, wants everything her way."

"Spoiled brat."

"Look at her, she thinks she's better than us."

"You think you're better than us, Michelle?"

But what I thought was that I wasn't good enough, that there must be something wrong with me to turn them all against me

31

so. I felt small and alone, scared of everything and completely misunderstood. So, I learned what I needed to learn in order to adapt. I learned to swallow my tears, bite my tongue and hide my feelings. I learned to push and shove with the rest of them and to shout out in anger when someone stepped on my toes. I learned to shrug my shoulders and laugh whenever tears threatened to well up in my eyes, and I learned to maneuver my way around the teasing and cruelty swarming through our unruly household.

Louis came to visit me from time to time, in the beginning, although Joan never did. I was never to see her again. I know now that she was simply unable to bear the thought, much less the sight, of me living in that run-down house, being raised by those people she considered unfit to have children. But Louis would drive up in his red truck, his blue eyes twinkling, and I would rush out to meet him, so glad he hadn't forgotten me. We would talk and laugh, although he wouldn't give me rides on his back any more and didn't tease me as much as he used to. I sensed that things had changed between us but I really didn't understand it; as far as I was concerned, he was still my Daddy. He was still the one who watched over me and taught me how to live in the world, giving me tender warnings and gentle advice whenever he saw me acting like a wild child.

Yet, I also had another daddy whom I was growing to love. My birth daddy, John.

John, who drank excessively and came home intoxicated and angry, scaring everyone in the house. John, who worked long hours away from home and who didn't want to talk about much of anything. John, moody and silent with his coffee and his western novels, slouching in his favorite chair while everyone tiptoed around him.

My birth daddy, John, who never said an unkind word to me, who allowed me to take his hand when he came home drunk and angry, and walk with him into the kitchen where he would make up a batch of his god-awful soup invention while everyone else in the house cowered behind locked doors careful not to make any loud noises.

I heard my brothers and sisters grumble about him, about how he hit them and yelled at them over the least little thing. I watched as my mother bit her lip in frustration when he would disregard her feelings and order her around. I saw these things, but I also saw something else, something that drew me close to him and made me love him fiercely. I saw a kindness in him, a yearning for a better life. I saw sadness in his brooding gaze as memories of a long-ago war washed over him, leaving him defeated and tired.

We didn't talk much during our times together. I would simply sit quietly beside him, exchanging looks of understanding with him every now and again. He didn't seem to wonder about how much I knew of his past life nor did I question him about it, but it was there with us, bonding us together in a silent, powerful way. Years later, I would discover that he had spent two years in a German prison camp during World War II after being a part of a specially-trained army unit under Colonel Darby in the First Ranger Battalion. It was at the Battle of Anzio in Italy where General Patton failed to make it through miles of mud and rain that my father's unit was captured by German troops. Many of his friends and comrades were killed during this battle as John watched in horror, fighting for his own life as well as theirs.

He was never to understand why he survived when so many of them didn't. He never talked much about what happened after that either, when he was tortured and starved and became seriously ill in the death camps of Germany, while being forced to witness the murders of many innocent Jews - the very people he had been fighting to save.

These memories forever raging in the back of his mind were the reason Vivian did her best to distract my father with a hundred different things, trying to make sure his needs were met, striving to keep her patience with his violent outbursts. The horrid memories of the war were also the reason John tried to distract himself any way he could, by drinking, by watching television or keeping the radio on - any kind of noise was better than silence. The silence haunted him, becoming a fertile ground for the worst of life's nightmares to come back into his conscious mind.

Maybe this was why we had such a strong connection; we were each plagued by our own demons, our own personal nightmares. His from long ago war memories and mine from nights of fitful sleep when I worried about seeing the future while crying and crying alone in the dark. We suffered through our secret tortures alone but the pain in our souls found solace in being together. Even though we didn't talk about it out loud, we shared an understanding of the silent anguish each of us experienced in our own way, and sometimes to be understood is the most comforting thing of all.

Each new nightmare during my childhood years brought me closer to John, changing me to be more and more like him in that I sought distractions in any way possible. We held a common dread of silence and of being alone. We didn't want to know what was swimming around in our heads. It was just too scary, too painful.

The idea that John might harm me in some way never entered my head. Of course he would love me, would be kind to me, would pat me affectionately on the head. That's what fathers did. I learned this from Louis. Louis, who gradually disappeared from my life as I grew closer and closer to John, and who let me go exactly when he was supposed to. For by the time he stopped coming around, I hardly even noticed his absence.

Baji: When one is tuned into the frequency of terror and fear and insecurity, this is what will be reflected in dreams. This doesn't mean that spirit help is unavailable; it is merely blocked by fears and can come through in a somewhat distorted manner. Michelle's intense curiosity about the future mingled with her deep fears stemming from early life experiences served to reveal future events to her in a most frightening way.

Each person is the creator of his or her own life experience here in the earth realm and will shape future activities according to the way one is viewing the world. Because Michelle was so fearful and mistrustful of life in general, and especially of herself, she was tuned into this type of vision where terror was in the forefront much of the time. Some children may have similar experiences with nightmares but without the premonitions simply because they are not so curious to know the future. Michelle happens to be one of those who relentlessly pursues information about what is coming, even though she is not always consciously aware of this!

These awful nightmares continued throughout most of my childhood, even though I tried everything I could think of to make them stop. However, it became a cycle of fear that only made matters worse and I was unable to control what happened to me in my dreams. But there were positive influences in my life as well, which served to balance things out to a certain extent. For one thing, there was Vivian, my mother, who laughed and laughed and made jokes out of everything. We got our clothes at the 'worn-a-bit' shop, she said, and our food at the 'chewed-a-bit' store. She cooked and cleaned and cleaned and cooked and swept our worries under rugs with her sharp wit and relentless energy. When troubles came our way, she would turn them into stories filled with humorous creatures and fantastic adventures. Sure, we could ride the dragon of hardship, she said, for we were warriors from another time, we were the endless brigade of East survivors; nothing would keep us down.

I used to wonder if she ever slept because it seemed she was always moving, always picking things up, putting things away, folding, ironing, stirring and mixing. She complained, oh yes she did, loud and clear, and she yelled at my father in a booming, angry voice. Many times, she chased after his ducking head with a hot iron or a glass bottle of some sort, intent upon breaking his skull because of his drunken behavior. She did not worry about keeping his dinner warm for him or about bathing his feet in warm water when he came home late at night tired and sore, weaving his way to the bedroom. But she did take care to protect her children from his hostile swings and shouts, placing herself in harm's way with a warrior stance, staring him down with her evil eye. I felt safe with her in the house, even though the place was in a constant uproar. I might get tossed about a bit from the rough ways of our world but Vivian made sure I didn't get broken, didn't get bruised enough to matter.

I loved her. I loved her warm hands on my hair, her hearty laughter in my ear and her warm oatmeal in my stomach. Thus, I became a full participant in my new existence, engaging in the day-to-day routines of a violent, crazy household, which was also filled with jokes and laughter, my little heart full with the love and pain of new family.

By the time I became an adult my perspective had changed quite a bit where dreams were concerned and with the help of Spirit I was able to glean messages from them - even when they came in the form of nightmares. For instance, when my mother-in-law, Arlene, appeared to me in a dream and said she was sick, I paid attention. In the dream she called to say she would not be able to sit with the kids that day since she wasn't feeling well. I was getting ready to go to work and felt immediate frustration as I now had to round up help elsewhere.

Arlene sounded okay to me, just a little under the weather, so I didn't think much of it. I left the house in search of my sister Pam, intending to ask her to sit with the kids instead. Why I didn't simply call her on the phone is a question only the dream beings can answer! Anyway, as I passed in front of Arlene's house across the street I saw a hearse in the driveway. Concerned, I asked one of the strange men standing in the driveway what was wrong and he told me that my mother-in-law was dead.

I remembered this dream so vividly, I felt sure it was a warning and took pains to keep a close eye on Arlene after that. She was sitting with the kids while I went to work but seemed in perfect health. Perhaps it was just a reflection of my own fears, I thought after weeks passed and nothing happened. By the time a year had passed, I had pretty much forgotten the whole thing until I answered the phone one morning to hear Arlene's voice on the line.

"I'm sorry, honey," she said, "but I won't be able to sit with the kids today. I'm just feeling so sick, I think I'll have to stay in bed."

Immediately, that long-ago dream rushed back into my mind and I knew I would not be going to work that day. Instead, I hurried across the street to insist Arlene let me drive her to the emergency room.

"Oh, it's not that bad," she protested. But I would not take no for an answer. Into the car she went, and I pressed the pedal hard to the floor. Before we had even reached the hospital, Arlene fell into a coma, which she did not emerge from for three days. Apparently, an aneurysm had burst behind her left eye, and as the doctors examined her, they found another one about to burst behind her right eye as well. If they had not done surgery so quickly, and if Arlene had not gone into the hospital that day, she would surely have died there at her house all alone.

Needless to say, I was very shook up! I became hyper-aware of my dreams, striving to pay attention to every detail. Now, instead of trying to block everything out like I had as a child, I was doing everything I could think of to make myself remember. So, when I started to have dreams about Arlene again, less than a month later, I *really* paid attention! In these dreams, her head seemed to be injured in some way. There were always bandages wrapped about her forehead area and sometimes I would see blood just below her hairline. Once again, I insisted she accompany me to the doctor.

"I'm fine," she protested, as before.

"You're not fine," I told her, emphatically.

"Really, Michelle. I'm just a little weak from the surgery still, that's all."

But I would not listen to this and planted her in front of the doctor, demanding he take a close look at her. He was none too impressed with my dream stories, however, and looked at me like I was some kind of kook just escaped from the loony bin. Still, I held firm and he was kind enough to oblige me since we had made the trip to see him, after all.

The moment he looked into Arlene's eyes with that little instrument of his, though, his feelings changed. He knew immediately that she was having a stroke. Fluid was building up inside her brain, unable to filter through her system correctly and quick action was needed to stop it, lest she die. A shunt was set in place to allow the fluid a drainage route, saving Arlene's life once again, much to our relief!

These incidents happened over ten years ago and except for being blind in one eye, Arlene has enjoyed a healthy life since, although neither of us has ever forgotten that frightening time. She is grateful, as I am, that those incredible dreams were not dismissed as the meaningless drivel of my unconscious. However, I also suspect that she had a hand in sending me those dreams as well, for she was not ready to die and wanted assistance in getting the help she needed. Sometimes, we call for help in a most unconscious way, our energy moving through the subtle arenas of our sleeping thoughts, carrying our intentions along the wings of Spirit.

Another time I was privy to information about the future, I was not so grateful, however. The premonition did not come through dreams that time but was planted into my head in a most forceful way even though I was not consciously looking for it at all. Our son Chris was seventeen and had been spending a lot of time with Matthew, a drifter from the city, who seemed unable to disentangle himself from a world of drugs and violence. I worried incessantly about his influence in Chris' life, although I liked Matthew immensely.

Chris was a daredevil during his teen years and caused me many moments of anxiety, which forced me to tune into the spirit realm for help more than I might have otherwise. His love for adventure often brought him into contact with other young people who were of a reckless nature, which didn't help matters in my view. In spite of my fears, however, I couldn't help but like his friends. They were usually wonderful spirits with a love for life and a penchant for fun. They made me laugh, which always wins me over right away.

Matthew was one such friend of Chris'. He was a wisecracking, humorous young man but was also a homeless teenager with little motivation toward bettering his life. However, it wasn't long after meeting him that he won my affection with his slow-spreading smile and quick wit.

One afternoon in May, Chris brought Matthew home with him, hoping I would agree to help his friend out. It seemed Matthew was desperate for a place to hang his hat. I learned that he had been living on the streets for four years, often going hungry as he bumbled his way along. It impressed me that he was so honest about his life, not blaming others for his predicament and acknowledging that he had little desire to get serious and hold down a respectable job.

"Okay," I told Chris, "he can stay for a couple of nights. But he's going to have to learn how to focus his energy so that his life isn't so chaotic."

"Thanks, Mom," Chris said, gratefully. He promised Matthew would not stay longer than a couple of nights. I felt good that I was able to provide shelter for Chris' friend that time, but I also worried a bit, remembering other such young people who would take advantage of kindness shown to them by stealing or by imposing themselves to an annoying degree.

But Matthew was very skilled at knowing when to come and when to leave. He stayed only two nights, as promised, that first time, but a few days later he showed up again, asking Chris if he could sleep on the sofa "just for tonight, bro".

He always thanked me profusely for my generosity and always ate sparingly as if afraid he was putting us out too much. In the morning his blankets would always be neatly folded on the end of the sofa. I certainly couldn't complain about his manners or behavior during those times when he was with us.

Still, I began to attach a feeling of dread to his visits after a while. I knew he was up to no good in the city when he was away and I was afraid my son would be inadvertently hurt by his association with him. I enlisted the help of my guides, asking them to show me what was underlying this feeling of dread I had whenever Matthew came around. It wasn't that I didn't like him, because I did. Always honest and open with me, he joked about his painful past and about his inability to hold a job. I tried to help him several times, getting him interviews with people, even getting him hired at a couple of places. But he always ended up right back in the same old predicament. It seemed to me he was unlucky, even though I did not believe in such a thing as blind luck. But his car would break down on the way to work, or he would catch a horrid flu and have to call in sick the second day of a new job; things like this would happen and he would get fired, even though it wasn't his fault. I couldn't understand it.

"I don't know how he is going to get out of that life," I told Bruce, despairingly.

My spirit guides helped me to calm down many times, encouraging me to stop and tune into the way my body was feeling. As I did this, I knew for certain that something awful was going to happen soon. It seemed to concern Matthew more than Chris, although I worried for my son's safety as well.

"You have to know there is something wrong," I told my son insistently. "Can't you feel it when you're around him?"

"I can't explain it to you, Mom," Chris said, shaking his head, "it's like we have this weird connection. I feel like he is my family and I can't desert him!"

I tuned in to my body and meditated alone in my room more and more frequently as the summer wore on, sure that Matthew was about to break our hearts in some way. What was he going to do? One day, while sitting in my room, I felt very strongly that Matthew was contemplating suicide. He had not been around for a few days and I was expecting him to show up at any time. Now, I wondered if we would ever see him again.

The next day, I warned Chris again that Matthew was going to hurt us in some way and asked if he had ever heard his friend talk about killing himself.

"No," Chris said, holding up a hand, "and don't start with me, Mom. Please."

I told him what I had felt the day before and he said he would check it out. Meanwhile, I worried. When Chris called later that day to assure me that Matthew was fine and I shouldn't be concerned, I felt no better, for I knew it was just a matter of time before something terrible happened.

"Try to forget about it," Bruce suggested, patting my shoulder comfortingly. "You've done everything you can to help that kid. He has to want to help himself, you know."

I knew Bruce was right, but I couldn't help but feel terrible. Matthew was such a sweet and lovable soul, so wise in his way. How could I just accept that something bad was going to happen to him? I wanted to help him, wanted to change what I knew was coming, but how? Nothing I did seemed to make any difference. Finally, I decided that Bruce was right and I should just let the whole thing go. Quietly, alone in my room, I turned it over to the spirit world, placing both Chris and Matthew into their hands.

About a week later, Matthew appeared at the door asking if he could spend the night. Nothing seemed different about him. It was a normal day like any other, but when he asked me that question, I heard something completely different inside my head.

I heard Matthew say he was going to kill himself. He was saying good-bye and expressing gratitude for all we had done for him. Shocked, I stared at him as he waited calmly for me to say yes he could stay, like I usually did.

"No, Matthew," I said, a catch in my voice, "I just can't keep on enabling you to live the way you live."

Even as the words came out of my mouth, I was overcome with remorse. What was I doing? The look on Matthew's face hurt me terribly and as he turned to leave, I knew that he was hurt, too. Where would he go? What would he do? I was beside myself with worry, wondering why I had heard such a terrible message in his innocent question. I took refuge in my bedroom, despite the oppressive temperature. It was late August and the heat had become nearly unbearable. Not having air conditioning usually kept me downstairs in the living room where the large trees in the front yard shaded the house and provided some relief, but at the moment I was desperate to be alone. I was also desperate for some spirit help; why weren't they helping me?

I heard and felt their calming messages but it was not enough. Nothing they said could soothe me, for I knew something awful was about to happen and now it felt as though I might be partly to blame for it.

"You shouldn't feel that way," Bruce insisted, when he came home from work and found me crying on our bed.

"But I turned him away," I wailed, "why did I do that?"

"Because you knew you weren't really helping him by letting him stay here," Bruce said.

I described my feelings of loss and despair to him, knowing they were connected to Matthew and Chris. No matter how I tried to think about it, I kept coming up with the same thing - something bad was coming. What if Chris were to be hurt, too? What if Matthew were to unwittingly drag my son into serious danger? I knew they sometimes hung around with kids who sold drugs and who got high and drove around the city much too fast - what if they were in a horrible car accident?

"You have to let go," Bruce said, gently.

"I did once but now it's all back again," I told him, sobbing. "It's all back now because I know that whatever it is that's going to happen is going to happen *soon!*"

"Well," Bruce said, rubbing my back, "whatever it is, Michelle, we'll get through it."

I wasn't so sure. Just the thought of losing Chris to some crazy teenage mishap filled me with terror. I couldn't lose him! I waited in agony until he came home late that night, and when he walked in the door, I descended upon him in a fury of fear.

"I don't know why you're so worried," he said, sighing. He informed me that Matthew was fine. He had heard that his friend was able to find someone else to take him in for the time being so it wasn't like he was sleeping on the streets.

"Did you see him tonight?" I asked.

"Naw. I'll prob'ly see him tomorrow, though. Go to bed, Mom, you look rough."

I sighed, kissing his cheek, and headed up to my room. At least Chris was home and safe, I thought. Whatever else was about to happen, at least I knew he was all right for now.

As I slept, my dreams came one after another. They were very disturbing and violent but each time I woke up I couldn't remember what I had been dreaming. The only parts I could recall were the horrible feelings of fear and sadness. In the morning I was so tired from all this dreaming and waking, I felt as if I hadn't slept at all.

Later, that same afternoon, we got the call. A girlfriend of Chris' told us what was already being broadcast in a special news report on television: Matthew had been involved in a shoot-out with two police officers. As I listened in horror, I realized immediately that a frightened Matthew had decided to end his life this way, lashing out at the society he had never felt a part of. In all the confusion, he had been shot by an understandably panicked police officer, right through the liver.

I felt as though I had been plunged into the depths of hell. If only I had let him spend the night! If only I hadn't turned him away... he would probably still be here, I thought, sitting in the front room with Chris watching television or something. Now, he was in the hospital fighting for his life. I tried hard to remember that all people choose when and how to exit this world, even if they don't realize it at the time. I had to keep in mind that Matthew was following his own life path - that he had known before he came here what road he wanted to travel on.

It is very, very difficult – often impossible - to remember this and be comforted by it when someone close to you has died, especially when it is under shocking and unexpected circumstances that they leave this earth. It makes no sense to us; we cannot understand it. I realized even then that the whole thing would look much different from a spirit's perspective but I was not a spirit; I was a human, and I was devastated.

Except that Matthew didn't die. Even though they thought he would and it looked as if he were about to at any moment, he pulled through and lived. He was slowly nursed back to health in the hospital, becoming stronger day by day - which he badly needed since he was now being charged with the premeditated attempted murder of two police officers.

During the trial that followed, I sat in the courtroom watching Matthew's sweet face trying to mask the fear he felt. Everyone in our family was grieving for him; we all felt awful that I had turned Matthew away that night. And, when the judge sentenced him to forty years in prison, I felt as if I would faint from the overwhelming grief that swept through me. How could I live with myself, knowing that this young man would be spending the better part of his life in prison? And me, with all of my previous experience with feelings of alienation and loss, how could I have turned him away when he needed me most?

When Chris came up to me later, I could hardly look at him, I felt so ashamed. But he placed a hand on my shoulder and spoke to me in that calm, soothing voice I love so much.

"I know this sounds crazy, Mom," he said, "but I feel like this whole thing has saved Matt's life."

I stared at him in disbelief. How could he say that? But he went on to explain to me things about Matthew that I had not known. Apparently, he was involved with many gang-related activities in the city and had been getting closer and closer to danger every day. Chris said he had worried that Matthew was going to be shot in a gang fight one of these days, he was getting so reckless. He also pointed out that if I had allowed Matthew to spend the night, Chris would have felt obliged to spend the next day with him so would probably have been with him during the shoot-out with police. As it was, he had been free to avoid Matthew that day, which he had been doing a lot of in recent weeks.

"He was just getting in too deep for me," Chris said, with a sigh, "but now I think he has a chance. At least he'll be alive."

I was greatly comforted by Chris' words. I hadn't known Matthew was so heavily involved in gang activities and I was just so grateful that my own son had the sense to back away when things got out of hand! Just thinking about him being so close to such danger set my teeth on edge. It was also a relief to hear that Matthew's sentence was reduced to twenty years and that, with good behavior, he was likely to receive parole in ten.

Matthew continues to write to us from prison even now. He thanks us, often, for our generosity and help during the many times when he needed it and holds no resentments about being turned away that last night. He is now taking college courses, working his way toward a bachelor's degree and is looking forward to a totally different life when he finally gets out of that place. I reminded him, not long ago, that he could have made this same choice while out here in the world, but he couldn't see things that way until he was put behind bars. I don't know why this was so for him but I hope he will take a look at it and work to figure it out.

As for me, I learned a great deal from knowing Matthew, and I am grateful to have him in my life. I learned that we cannot control another's destiny or life-path; each must decide this for him or her self. I also learned that not everyone will take the easiest road - many times we don't. For some reason or another, we choose to get hit over the head time and again because of some lack of insight or blocked intuition. Why is this so? I have asked my guides this many times, hoping to avoid such patterns in my own future. What I get from them is the very important point that we must look within, first and foremost, within the deep universe of our own nature. The answers are all in there. We must pay attention to the way we feel, and meditate on why we are feeling that way. We should look back over our experiences and pick out those things that seem to keep affecting us and learn the lessons we came here to learn.

The more we keep our minds and hearts open, the less we inhibit our own growth and the more we can answer the call of our own spirits to go forward and thrive in this world.

Most of us have had the experience of someone calling us or knocking on the door just after we were thinking about them. Many times, we may not even realize we had a premonition of something until it happens. Then, we think back and remember that, yes, we were thinking about that or we did have a vague feeling this or that was going to happen. The fact that this is so common only goes to show that it is a natural part of being human. It is a normal aspect of our physical lives here on earth. So why don't we pay more attention to it? Why don't we focus more on the intuitive responses within ourselves and act on this wisdom? We have been taught to doubt ourselves and to ignore the messages coming from within.

Children do not seem to be as torn about such things, especially if they are taught to trust in their own sense of reality. It is only through the reactions of others that they will learn to block the wisdom of their intuition. I was frightened by premonitions when I was young because the people around me reacted to my predictions and insights with fear and ridicule. As a result, when my own children were born, I was determined that they would feel no such pressure no matter how bizarre their insights sounded.

We began to notice early on that our son Chris had a very developed sensory perception and was quick to pick up on things the rest of us missed. He was too little to be working on the development of such skills; they just came naturally to him. I was especially excited when I noticed that he would sometimes make a comment about something that hadn't happened yet.

"Chuck boke," he said one day as I carried him out onto the front porch. We waved at Stan, one of Bruce's friends, who was pulling up to the curb in his old pickup truck.

"Hey there," Stan said, cheerily. He sauntered up the steps and ruffled the top of Chris's head. "How's my guy?"

"Chuck's boke," Chris said, pointing at Stan's pickup truck.

"He's telling you your truck is broken," I said, laughing.

Stan snorted. "Sure looks broke, don't it? Rusty piece of junk. Gets me around, though."

Later, after he and Bruce had pulled away in that old truck, Chris told me again that the truck was 'boke.'

"Well, it sure is old and ugly," I told him.

"Yeah," he said, grinning, "chuck's boke."

Sure enough, less than an hour later, Bruce called to say that he and Stan were stranded on the side of the road and needed a ride. Apparently, a rear axle had broken on the truck and they were unable to go any further.

"Guess it's ready for the trash heap," Bruce said, with a chuckle.

I realized then that Chris had somehow sensed the truck was broken, even though he couldn't articulate *how* he knew. Even as adults it is often difficult for us to explain *how* we know something intuitively. We just *know*. So, why don't we count on our intuition more? Why don't we trust what our own feelings and senses tell us and why is it so easy to get mixed up about what our intuition is saying, exactly?

Baji: You have all the answers you need right there inside of you. There is no need to fret about what others are saying or doing. Just stop and listen; you are a part of a greater and wiser system than you realize.

Past experiences and the influences of others who are bound by their own past experiences serve often to separate you from the whisperings of wisdom your intuition and soul can send you. This is why it is often difficult at first for people to understand what their true selves are saying to them. Also, it is hard for a person to hear the advice and guidance and insight of those in his or her Spirit Circle if he or she is not even aware that such a support system exists!

Still, there is a general acceptance of such things as 'gut reactions' and 'playing out a hunch' and 'just having a feeling' about certain things. This shows that people do recognize the validity of such responses. What more people would do well to remember, however, is that these occurrences needn't be so rare. They can become a natural way of living life, each and every day. Again, the key is to simply pay attention. You are getting tons of information all the time through dreams, feelings, twinges in the gut, sparks in the mind... all you have to do is become more alert. Watch, listen, feel, remember - and above all, trust what you get.

With practice, you will get better and better at sifting out the truth of your soul from the nonsense of the world. But don't get too impatient or frustrated with the nonsense either, for it is an exciting part of the earthly adventure, too! Resolve to detect the difference bit by bit, day by day, for this will make your human life easier. Most people are seeking to improve their lives in some way, and paying attention to your inner voice will always work toward this end. Just don't be in too much of a hurry, for the search itself is a necessary and important part of your divine plan. *Enjoy and appreciate as you go. Relish the sorting and the figuring out and the moments of awakening to Self. It's not how fast you get 'there' that matters so much as the intention to embark upon the journey in the first place!*

Michelie Senjem and Rebecca LeTourneau

The Night Owl Searches

There life never slows
The hillside at night
It has soft shadows moving
Over yesterday's snow

The stars high, shine in our eyes.
And the wind howls, then it cries

There the night owl searches
Alone in the sky
With the light of the moon

In that twilight
We with our hearts
Art alone with nature
Are alone in the dark

Beauty of soul these nights
Planned in heaven, brought down in beams
We live these nights, covered with trees
Naked in light all that is seen

In the mind's life
Shadows never meet
Our minds and our beings
Are never erased

There the night owl searches
Alone in the sky
With the light of the moon.

— Mike East

Michelle Senjem and Rebecca LeTourneau

Floundering in Hell's Kitchen

"Why can't I seem to help those closest to me?" I asked Baji one day. It was a time of discouragement, for I felt as though everything I did turned against me - at least when it came to dealing with family members and close friends. There was no easy way to tell the ones who needed to hear it that they had a problem with drugs and alcohol. There was no clear speech I could think of that would open their eyes to the realities of their own lives. Didn't they see how they were sabotaging their relationships? Didn't they notice how much they were hurting others?

I couldn't seem to come up with an effective way to reach these people; couldn't seem to get across to them that they were traveling down a difficult road that would kill them if they didn't stop and turn around soon. I wanted to scream it in their faces, some of them, like my good friend Karen, or my longtime gal pal Suzy, or even some of my siblings. I wanted to shake them loose from the grip of substance abuse; hadn't they learned their lesson by watching our father? Didn't Karen and Suzy have a yearning to be different from their own alcoholic parents?

The fact that I couldn't seem to make a difference infuriated me. I was beside myself with anxiety and anger. Karen couldn't seem to keep her electricity bill paid, and Suzy was going through men like crazy, threatening to kill herself every time one of them left. These were not the beautiful fun-loving friends I remembered. Something had obviously happened to them along the way and of course I knew what that was... it was the drinking and the pot smoking and the denial of sobriety. They were turning into mush right before my eyes and there was nothing I could do about it. Unbelievably frustrated, I called upon Baji with desperation.

53

You must go where your interests pull you, Michelle. Stop and pay attention to what your body is telling you. What are you feeling? Do you really want to go down to the bar and sit there while Suzy cries about her life to you? Do you really want to have Karen whining in your kitchen about her bills while showing you the latest designer clothes she just bought?

What do you really want? What do you feel like doing?

A part of me wanted to cut them out of my life. Who needed the aggravation? But another part of me remembered the love I felt for these two. I felt the loyal tugging of our past friendships and felt I couldn't fully abandon them. Baji kept asking me questions until I found myself deciding that I wouldn't cut them out completely but would follow my feelings moment by moment. If I didn't want to do something at a particular time when one of them called, I wouldn't do it. This was going to be my biggest challenge, I knew, for it would be difficult to tell them 'no', even if their feelings were hurt. But I had to be true and faithful to my own spirit first - to my own intuition.

At first, the girls had fits, each in their own way. Karen told me off and threatened to never speak to me again, saying I had changed, I thought I was better than her, boy I sure forgot where I came from didn't I... and Suzy just cried and cried, leaving tearful messages on my answering machine, accusing me of abandoning her. I explained to both of them that I simply had to live by my own instincts. I tried to get across to them how my life had changed over the years, how substance abuse was no longer something I was interested in, and how my spirit guides now worked with me to improve my outlook on life. They were not convinced, and remained upset but as time went on and I held firmly to my convictions, they gradually came to accept our friendship on new terms. I would communicate with them on my own terms. There were no guarantees. That meant I would not be sitting with them down at the bar, I would not allow them in my house to chitchat unless I was in the mood, and if they got too obnoxious it might be months before I would feel like seeing them again.

Of course, they thought I had gotten incredibly stuck up! But they also seemed to realize that something wonderful and strengthening had happened to me and I think they wanted to have it, too. For they knew I was still the same person who loved them unconditionally, who laughed at their jokes and sympathized with their problems. They began to realize that I still cared but had learned to put myself first. My own path had become the most important one and they respected this, however reluctantly. I knew they wondered how I was able to pull it off. They had been trained, as I had, that women should fuss after the world, picking up the lint of others' despair, working and bending and shifting and scuffling to set things right again for everyone else but themselves. Karen and Suzy drank and smoked pot so they wouldn't have to think about the lint of others, so they could forget for a few hours. But once they were sober again, boy, they were out there running around like crazy women, searching for that lint to pick up.

What still bothered me, though, was wondering why on earth a spirit would choose to come into human form only to chase around and around in destructive circles for an entire lifetime. Why would someone come to this earth just to live and die as an alcoholic? It seemed so pointless, somehow, such a waste of time and energy.

Baji: Some people are really addicted to feeling certain things. Some human personalities are very absorbed in many of the different things offered here in the earth realm and pay very little attention to their spiritual connections. Spirit doesn't really have a lot of opinion about that. As a human, you may see some things as very detrimental to someone's health but Spirit doesn't look at it in this same light. Spirit takes all knowledge, absorbs it, and moves forward.

You have to remember that the person experiencing the revolving door effect is not the only opportunity his or her nature has to expand its awareness. There are many more dimensions to every soul than those you see in your earthly form.

Spirit will allow such freedoms and is very patient, as well as very willing to love you no matter what your interest may be. At some spiritual level, every soul knows what it is doing. One's reasons to be interested in suffering may be as varied and important as another's reasons to be interested in spreading joy around. The more you understand suffering, for instance, the better you become at creating solutions for every scenario. So, everything has its rewards and everything is useful to Spirit whether it is simply amusing or is used as an incredible stepping-stone for expansion.

You need to honor your feelings of withdrawal from sections of life which do not interest you, for this is how you can further your own spiritual quest for creativity. But this does not mean that someone else's path isn't just as valid and needed, even when it appears counterproductive, for those experiences are useful to the journey of another soul and are in alignment with the interests of a different nature in this time frame. We all live long enough to experience every angle, every approach to life because we are eternal, you see. What do you suppose this means? Eternity is eternity; time constraints are non-existent. So, while you have put yourself into a limited time frame for the span of a physical life, this does not mean you are limited at the soul level, for you are not. And, what is holding one person's interest at the moment may not be holding yours, but this is only because they are engrossed in a different activity at the moment. Nothing is useless, it all becomes part of an incredible pattern of knowledge which all can share and draw upon for all time, moving everything forward.

You may have decided that Suzy visits that corner bar way too often and that she is bound to end up in a bad place or with a worthless existence, but you should remember that your vision is limited while you are here in this physical realm. Suzy may be riding out twists and turns that will form a pattern much needed in the future, because in time even the worst of messes can become something creative and necessary. Take yourself where you wish to go, learning and growing for us all, but love Suzy. She has different interests than you right now; that is all.

During those days when I was exploring my feelings on this issue, Mija came to me and whispered into my ear something about Karen and Suzy not being the only ones. I was confused. Not the only ones what? I could feel Mija's gentle laughter as she sent memories swirling inside my head: memories of a young teenage girl named Michelle who appeared to have made it her mission in life to destroy herself. My two old friends, and some of my siblings, were not the only ones who had chosen to walk a destructive path. I had traveled that road myself once, and had been untouchable at the time. No one could reach me with any type of wisdom; I had a mind of my own and my mind was intent upon destructive behaviors and thought patterns. That was that.

As I recalled those years, and all those who had tried to help me, I felt embarrassed that I had been so quick to judge Suzy and Karen and the others. They were still in that place, still in that world I had left behind, but because I was once a part of it, I should have understood what held them there. After all, what had held *me* there for so long? No one can or will come out of that kind of a situation until their inner self has agreed to change. Otherwise, it is just blowing in the wind to try and get them to crawl out of it. This is not to say we shouldn't try to help people who have these types of problems but we need to be listening to our intuition as we attempt such things, for if the person is not willing to participate in his or her own salvation, the rescue will not be successful.

I couldn't believe the things I had done and the way I felt about life when I was younger. Why had I been so destructive? It hurt me to think back to those years. I was so lost, so confused and disconnected. Why would I choose to engage in such a lonely adolescence?

It seemed I was forever tuning in to sorrow, pain, and death during my younger years. Even as I prayed for blissful silent sleep, the dreams would come and in the morning I would know that a relationship was about to end or someone was going to be injured in some kind of fall, or some other unhappy event was bound to occur. There I would be, sitting in my bed as the sun was just beginning to peep through the windows, already filled with dread and anxiety before the day had even begun.

Other times, I would see things in broad daylight with my eyes wide open. I would see what others could not - angry faces behind someone's head or blood oozing out of someone's arm, even though there was no blood there.

These visions scared me because I knew I would hear at some point that this one had been beaten up by his parents or that one had cut open a gash in her arm while climbing a neighbor's fence. And, I would know that I had seen it first - before it happened. Yet I didn't see things clearly enough or understand things well enough to warn people in advance. I couldn't stop these things from happening, so what good were these visions and dreams? It seemed to me they served no purpose but to torture me and I resented them. I resented how they made me feel, so frightened and helpless, and I resented the way others treated me because of them.

"Don't say anything about us, Michelle," my brothers and sisters would say, as if my very words could cause something disastrous to happen. I began to keep more and more of these psychic experiences secret, hoping people would forget all about them. The world seemed to work in a way contrary to my feelings and senses. People said things that I knew were not true, and would often do things in opposition to what they really wanted - it was all very confusing.

Often, I wished I couldn't see the truth behind words and actions; I didn't want to receive information I had not asked for. I didn't want to know when something bad was about to happen, either. I didn't want to pick up on the negative feelings of others, didn't want to run into their insecurities and fears inside my own mind. With all of my might, I resisted any type of extrasensory information and finally, around the time I reached puberty, things began to slow down for me in this area.

Still, all the energy spent in trying to be 'normal' had pretty much exhausted me by this time. My natural instincts and intuition had been suppressed so much that by the time I reached my teen years, I was thoroughly confused. I was so nervous and stressed out, both because of my own efforts to look and act like everyone else, and because of the feelings I was picking up from others, that it became a laborious chore just to get myself through the day. There was no room, no free space left, in which my authentic self could emerge. I had beaten it down with a fierce determination until it became deeply hidden beneath my strained smiles and careless chatter, and even I could not remember what it was like.

Being blond, pretty, and well developed for my age brought me lots of attention from members of the opposite sex, often from men much older than myself, and I was hungry for love and attention. I craved, desperately, to be treasured again as my foster parents had treasured me so long ago and when those good looking young men told me I was so beautiful and so special, I chose to believe them. I imagined them sincere as they gazed at me in a way that suggested I was the most important being in the world to them. I listened to their sweet whisperings and melted into Cinderella fantasies, one after the other. Before long, sex had become a routine part of my life.

The bond I had with my father, which had been so strong during my early years, began to weaken. Years of heavy drinking had taken their toll, making John increasingly unavailable to all of us. He withdrew more and more into his own misery, emerging only now and again to bark at us in anger, his rage always incredibly out of proportion to whatever he was yelling about. I began to stay out of his way, just as my brothers and sisters did, avoiding him more and more simply because I was tired of his despair. It no longer held me to him, for my own misery had grown so deep and so large I was no longer able to deal with his.

So, I turned to boys and, sometimes, to men twice my age. I turned to those who showered me with attention, who professed to understand and appreciate me. Young, insecure, and hopelessly lost, I chose to believe their urgent ramblings, giving them what they wanted even though I knew deep down it was all an illusion.

My self-esteem withered away to nothing as prince after prince turned out to be nothing but an ugly frog. It became harder and harder to fool myself into believing that I was special and beautiful. Instead I started to think badly of myself. What were people saying about me behind my back?

People told me I was lucky, being blond and gorgeous, but to me this was not a gift. It only served to fill me with heaviness and guilt. I walked around with a wooden smile, an empty shell of a girl, hiding the fact that I could hardly stand being in my own skin any more.

Drugs helped. They made it easier to pretend. So did alcohol. I began to drink and get high as often as I could, trying to block out feelings, hunches, and premonitions. School became a place to buy drugs or to meet with friends who would share what they had with me. I rarely attended classes any more, choosing instead to take off and party someplace, numbing myself any way I could.

However, the drugs sometimes triggered things in my mind I had been trying to avoid for a long time. I would see images around me and around others or I would hear whispers and would fly into a panic.

"Oh god, she's freaking out again," the kids would tell each other as I crouched in some corner, paralyzed with fear. They would take turns sitting with me, telling me it was just the drugs, just a bad trip, nothing to get upset about. I wanted to believe them but I had memories of other times... other visions and dreams... and I had not been doing drugs back then.

My only relief came when the drugs and alcohol numbed me into a peaceful, uninterrupted silence and everything was blocked out. These were the times I lived for. These were the moments of relief that kept me going back time and again, money in hand, searching for someone to sell me some pot or pills, anything to quiet my disturbing thoughts.

I was just thirteen years old the first time I attempted to take my own life. My father had finally turned his rage and irrational violence toward me and threw me out of the house, accusing me of looking like my mother, of all things. It was so hard to believe he was actually addressing me that I simply stood there in the living room staring at him in disbelief.

"I said get the hell out!" he roared, slamming his fist into the wall next to my head. I fled to my sister Pam's house across town and sobbed onto her kitchen table as she tried to understand why I was so shocked.

"He's always been crazy," she said, patting my back.

Yes, I thought, but not toward *me*. This is what hurt most of all. I had always thought myself exempt from John's hatred but now I truly was like the rest of my siblings, for our father had rejected me as well.

I lived with Pam after that but felt no joy in my newfound freedom. I could come and go pretty much as I pleased and all my friends were envious of me but I had descended to a place of no feeling at all. Even getting up in the morning seemed a chore. Getting dressed seemed pointless. Going to school seemed like an absolute joke. So, one morning I decided life just wasn't worth the trouble and slit my wrists with a razor blade.

"Do you really want to die, Michelle?"

The doctor stood over me in a white coat, a stern expression on his face. It was a question that would be put to me many times over the next couple of years.

"Why do you keep trying to take your life?"

"Why don't you want to live?"

"You don't really want to die, do you?"

But I didn't know the answer to these questions. I couldn't even comprehend the questions themselves. All I knew was that I was in the hospital again and again, still alive, which meant the charade would have to continue. Back to school, back to the social scene, back to the pasted-on smile and the act my life had become. So, each time I was set free again I headed straight back to the drugs and alcohol, anxious to numb myself any way I could.

One day, I had been drinking with some girlfriends behind the school building when a group of boys walked by, capturing our attention. I recognized one of them and called out to him.

"Kenny!"

He turned, his frown giving way to a wide, flashing smile when he saw me waving.

"Hey, funny girl. What's going on?"

I laughed, breaking away from my friends to stumble across the parking lot to where he stood, tall and handsome, his hands reaching out to steady me.

"Whoa there, girl, how much have you had to drink?"

"Not much. Whaddya got today, anything good?"

"Not really, just some downers."

"Yeah? Lemme see."

"Sure."

Kenny quickly became all business as he pulled a small baggy out of his pocket. I leaned into him, squinting to see the tiny white pills inside.

"Thas' all?"

Kenny chuckled. "There are lots of highs in here, funny girl. But it's going to cost you."

"Yeah, yeah."

I fumbled around in my school bag until I found the crumpled wad of bills at the bottom.

"Here," I said, "now, gimme those, will ya?"

I snatched the baggy from his hand and started popping pills into my mouth.

"Hey," Kenny protested, "let me count this first."

He concentrated on the money in his hand as I cleaned out the baggy and turned back toward my friends who were watching me and giggling.

"Okay," Kenny called after me, "looks about right. Just don't take 'em all at once, funny girl."

I waved over my shoulder while trying to aim my feet in the right direction.

"See ya," I said, smirking at one of my girlfriends who was practically drooling over the sight of Kenny behind me.

"He's so cute," she said as I grew near. I waved a hand in his direction, acting nonchalant.

"He's okay."

"We'd better get back," someone else said after a bit. I felt a tug on my arm. I didn't understand why they felt it necessary to go to class all of a sudden but it had become too difficult to speak so I simply went along, following the others into the building.

It was wonderful not to care about anything. Go to school, don't go to school, I didn't care one way or the other. Be with friends, be alone, what difference did it make? I was dizzy and floating... floating along. Where... where had the others gone? I couldn't remember saying good-bye to them, couldn't remember taking a different path. I had a class somewhere down this hall... or that one...

I'm on the floor, I thought, dully. I'm lying on the floor... or am I floating above it?

There was the sound of rushing feet, screeching rubber against the polished floor... running... then, voices all around me, excited voices... but they were getting farther and farther away... someone was patting my cheek... so many faces over me, but I didn't recognize them... did I? I felt myself leaving them, easily drifting away... until, finally, a blessed darkness embraced me, and I was gone.

"Why do you want to die, Michelle?"

There I was again, not dead, not gone. I was in the hospital with people around me asking questions. Somehow, I mustered up the strength to respond to them. I slipped back into my play-acting mode and told them what they wanted to hear.

Yes, I understood what had happened. No, I didn't realize how dangerous it was. Yes, I wanted to live. No, I would never do anything like that again. Blah, blah, blah. How stupid, I thought. Words were just words; they didn't mean anything. People would believe what they wanted to believe. I let them think they had convinced me to turn my life around, that they had made a difference. Anything to get out of there.

As was hospital policy, a nurse escorted me to the door in a wheelchair. I held my throbbing head and thought about how ridiculous life was. The hall grew crowded as we neared the emergency room doors and I sighed with impatience. It would be much easier to just get up and walk! But I had to follow the rules, had to play the part of the good girl for the time being, so I sat quietly and chewed on my lower lip.

As the nurse who was pushing me slowed to let some people pass, I happened to glance across the hall to where a teenage boy was crumpled in his own wheelchair, moaning in pain. His face was covered with blood.

"Ugh," I said, without thinking. The sound of my voice caused him to look up in my direction and when he did, I gasped in shock.

"Kenny!"

He was whisked away just at the instant our eyes met, disappearing behind the emergency room doors, but not before the image of his badly cut, bloody face was burned forever into my memory.

Kenny had gone through a windshield that day. He had been high on the very same drug he had sold me and got over one hundred stitches in his once handsome face because of it. I was so sorry for him but did not realize the significance of this strange meeting in the hallway of the hospital. I would not let myself believe that it was some sort of sign, some kind of warning. For years I had been fighting desperately to escape just this sort of thinking so even when it came at me in the form of blatant coincidences I refused to take heed.

I kept taking drugs. In fact, I took the same drug again, and this time I went through a windshield myself! Another sign. Another warning that I closed my eyes and heart to, blocking out every thought that might open up those psychic doors again. Cut and bruised, I shrugged it off and went right back to my wild ways. Except that it was getting harder and harder to get my hands on drugs. News of my suicide attempts, car accidents, and my overdose had gotten around and nobody wanted to be responsible for putting me in my grave.

"Don't give her any," they told each other, "she can't handle it."

"No, Michelle, I won't sell to you - you're suicidal!"

"What's wrong with you - you got a death wish or something?"

But I just laughed at these remarks, dismissing the concerns of my friends and siblings with a flippant wave of my hand. If I couldn't do drugs, I'd just drink more. As long as I could surround myself with people and fun, I didn't have to think. I surely didn't want to think too deeply about anything. I didn't want to dream either, not if I could help it. So I drank and ran around, laughing and joking and having as much fun as I could. At least I called it fun, but it was really an attempt to keep myself as preoccupied as possible so I wouldn't have a chance to see what was going on inside.

But there were always those moments when I would find myself alone and sober. Inevitably, these times would come and I would have to face myself. These were the worst and most frightening times for me. I would stand there looking at my reflection in the mirror and would have to fight off the panic. Who was I? Certainly not that girl in the mirror, she was a stranger to me.

Stubborn and desperate, I tried one more time to end my physical life. After hours of drinking at a friend's house, I stumbled into the garage, car keys in hand. A dim recollection of something somebody had said once made me think to prop a snowboard up against the exhaust pipe before climbing behind the wheel.

"Okay," I said aloud, as I started the engine. This time it would work. I made sure all the windows were rolled up and then lay down in the front seat, my head swimming, and waited to die.

It should have been so easy. Who would think to look for me in the garage? Everyone was drunk, carrying on in the house with the music blaring as laughter rose out of the open windows and into the night. No one would imagine that Michelle had gone off to die quietly and alone in a parked car.

Well, as it turned out, no one did imagine this. No one even missed me, really. But my brother Mark just happened by, seeking somewhere to make out with his girlfriend, and saw me there lying motionless in the front seat. He didn't try to wake me up, just turned off the engine and rolled down one of the windows so I could sleep in peace until morning. So, when I woke up the next day, there I was fully alive, hangover and all. Confused, I sat up, clutching my aching head. I saw the window rolled down. The keys were gone and the car was turned off. Who had done that?

Even as I wondered this, the realization of what I had tried to do the night before hit me and a sharp stab of fear raced through my chest. Jesus, I tried it again! I couldn't remember making the decision to end my life this time; why had I done it? Did something happen? But nothing seemed out of the ordinary as I tried to retrace my steps the previous day. We had all been laughing and drinking like we usually did. There hadn't been any arguments, any conflicts. I felt the fear wash over me again as I pictured myself in the front seat, never waking up again, just lying there dead and still like a mannequin. I sat there, somewhat surprised by this fear and that's when it dawned on me that I didn't want to die after all. This was a revelation in itself, for I had never been sure before. I thought of all the times people had asked me those questions and I could never think of what to say because I just didn't know.

"Do you want to die, Michelle?"

"No!" I said, aloud, to the stillness of the car.

The sound of my own voice surprised me and I became very still, lost in thought. I could have died so many times; why didn't I? For some reason, I was always pulled back, rescued just in time. No matter how much I tried to sabotage myself, it seemed some invisible force greater than myself was protecting me. Apparently, there was a purpose for my being on this earth, alive and breathing.

Many, many signs that I had ignored over the past couple of years began to come back to me then, one after another. I was stunned as I recognized the connections between strange coincidences that had happened to me so many times. Kenny and me, both in wheelchairs, both going through windshields after taking the same drug, near-misses of death, running into people in odd places, things certain people had said... it all came together for me into one awe-inspiring moment of perfect clarity.

"Well, okay," I said. I stopped, for the first time in years, and totally relaxed. I let down my defenses and allowed myself to feel the presence of spirits around me. Tired of the struggle, I gave up, raising my hands in a gesture of defeat. It seemed there was no use in trying to escape, in trying to end my life, for none of these attempts ever worked anyway. I heaved a deep sigh and climbed out of the car, my head still throbbing. If I wasn't going to kill myself, if I was going to keep on living on this crazy planet, I thought, then I might as well try to be happy!

This defeat of mine, this giving up, became a catalyst for me. Over the next several months, I began to see life in a different light. Certainly, I was not yet fully happy, nor was I consciously intent upon drastically changing my life. But at least I had learned to turn things over to the universe to a certain extent; I was no longer trying to be in sole control of my every experience. Slowly, I began to release my fears and anxieties into the spirit world, hoping at some vague level it would take care of me. I didn't seek out drugs any more since they only freaked me out anyway. I also didn't try to kill myself any more, figuring it just wasn't in the cards for me; apparently something or someone needed me alive. I did continue to drink sometimes, though, and hang out with a party crowd but even in doing this I began to practice more moderation. Drunkenness really brought me no joy and no relief, so what good did it do?

During these somewhat confusing times, I was repeatedly drawn to the spirit world, to the mystical side of life. Because of the many coincidences that saved my life, I began to wonder about life after death and about other dimensions. I wondered why I could see and hear things sometimes, even while sober, and why I had always been able to sense the thoughts and feelings of those around me. Instead of being so afraid, however, I began to find myself more and more curious. After all, this spirit world I seemed to be connected to couldn't be all bad since it had often kept me from killing myself!

Gradually, I began to trust what I could not see. As this trust grew, the connection seemed to grow stronger between the invisible world and myself and as this connection grew stronger, I grew happier. It didn't happen all at once, but things began to occur in my life that caused me joy and laughter, even though I hadn't been trying to make this sort of thing happen. It just did. I now know that simple joy in being is a natural by-product of relating to your most natural and eternal self, which is what I was beginning to do at that time, even though I didn't consciously realize it. These connections to the spirit world had always been there at the edges of my conscious awareness, ever since I could remember. So, when I stopped trying to deny this fact, I was able to function much more naturally and more in accordance with my authentic way of being. When this happened, as it will with anyone, the universal energy began to flow more easily in my favor.

Just as I opened the channels that had been blocked for so long within myself, so did the channels open for me in the world, which had so long seemed inaccessible. My life was not simply a burden or a chore; it was an avenue to happiness and joy. At first, I just suspected this might be true and dared to hope, but soon I was to discover the absolute truth of it and would leave my doubting, suicidal self behind forever.

Baji: *Michelle certainly did experience much of the wildness this planet has to offer. We continually tried to capture her attention and lead her back to a more inquisitive state but the more she drank and the more drugs she did, the harder it was for her to hear us. There are many, many distractions for humans; many things that can divert one's attention away from the spirit realm and from what their own spiritual journey is all about. But this isn't to say that the diversion activities are not valuable to the spirit realm, and to the person's soul level, for they are.*

Nothing is ever wasted in spirit. Whatever one is doing, the information of that experience is kept for all time and serves all of existence. For the individual in question, these diversions only mean it will take them longer to get to the lessons and adventures they intended to engage in while here on the earth realm. At the soul level, each knows that there is no time

69

Michelle Senjem and Rebecca LeTourneau

constraint to learning; whatever is not looked at this time around can always be addressed later. But, at the human level, these distractions may induce unnecessary suffering, for when one is cut off from his or her spiritual intentions, the flow will not be as easy, life will not be in alignment with the soul desires, and conflict occurs. This is often what is happening when humans feel they are experiencing a 'brick wall' effect, where no matter what they try or what they do, it just doesn't work out and they end up in misery again. This is a clue, to those who want to see it, that your life is not in alignment with your soul intentions. Something is distracting you. What is it? Sometimes, the distractions themselves are interesting enough to be included as lessons in the spiritual journey of this particular lifetime; other times they are merely distractions, meaningless to your current life, and you should just go on and forget them quickly.

Michelle did indeed learn much through her teen years and has gained valuable insights through those experiences, but they were not necessary for her to go through, at least not so much as she thinks they were sometimes. Who she is now, and what her life is about now, would have come about anyway, for it was in her all the time, waiting. She could have experienced healthy and happy teen years and still arrived at exactly where she is now, as far as soul development goes. Her creative growth was not dependent upon her going through some specific trauma as a teen and has not even been affected by this so much as by other, often happier, experiences. But she chose that path at that time, for her interests led her away from the reasons she came here.

Still, it is helpful to remember that this wayward meandering is expected, and is known to be a normal part of the human experience. While still in spirit form, you know that you are going to get side-tracked while in the earth realm, you know that your focus will not be as intense as when you are in spirit. This is part of the attractiveness of the human adventure! It is like play time, as well as work time, even when a life is filled with crazy misfortunes. From the spirit perspective, it is all interesting in the same way; there is no distinction between happy and sad, painful and joyful, as far as value is concerned. At the spirit level, it is all equally valuable. The subject of all spirit study is LOVE, and with all the different experiences gained through different types of existence, such as a human existence, our understanding of love deepens and grows and expands.

Thus, love becomes like the sun is to humans, an ever-burning, self-perpetuating life force which can always be studied a bit more, can always be understood just a little better, because there is always more to it, always another side to it, another dimension, a deeper meaning. Love is the most incredible essence in existence - it IS existence, yet it is infinite, which means it will be forever studied and sought after and yearned for in an ever-deepening way. Spirit yearns for a deeper understanding of love just as humans do, although one can understand and experience a different dimension of love while in spirit than one can in the human realm, and vice versa! We all want it, we all search for it, we all study it to know more about it, we all try to live in it, acquire it, share it, keep it, hold onto it, and so forth. Love is what lies behind our desire to create, for CREATING is LOVE IN ACTION.

The act of creating is an act based in love, even though this creative talent, which is divine in its essence, can be used toward evil intent. But the very act of creating is, in itself, pure divinity.

However, an interesting thing happens when humans get sidetracked and participate in things that weren't particularly necessary. This is one of the most profound miracles of life, actually, for as I said, nothing is wasted. When one goes down a destructive path and finds oneself in unwelcome situations, regretful incidents and so forth, it affects the patterns of the universe nonetheless. Paths cross, looks are exchanged, lives are touched and affected, messages penetrate the unconscious and spirit plans are reinforced. For instance, even though Michelle did not have to engage in such destructive activities when she was young, the fact that she did served to propel other forces forward, adding to the overall knowledge and expansion of the planet. She became a part of the memory of those whom she affected. People remember her as a young girl, as a teenager; perhaps something she said or did affected how they thought about things later on, shaped the words they spoke to others, etc.

The spiritual searching of others can draw upon those memories of Michelle, even during her destructive years, and mold these memories into a tool to further their own spiritual journey. At the human level, you can never know how much you are affecting others, even strangers, and cannot see how even a glance or a smile or an overheard remark can set entire life paths in motion. It is absolutely amazing how much this happens. It all fits together, destructive or not, to form another level of existence, another stepping-stone in overall expansion.

Everything swirls around everything else, moving and dancing, experience fitting into experience, thought forming thought, to create a massive movement forward, always forward, ever-expanding and growing and creating into the future. This is why regret is so unnecessary. One person may feel awful about something they did in the past; they may be consumed with guilt about something, but these feelings should be released and trust restored, for everything is used, everything fuels the movement forward, and all is eventually turned around in pursuit of LOVE.

If you are ashamed of things in your past, let it go. Realize that somewhere, somehow, Spirit made something good out of it, and will continue to do so. The negative effects of anything are usually felt more at the human level, which is why people can end up harming themselves in the physical realm, because Spirit cannot really be hurt. Doing bad things, or hurting others, will not damage anything at the soul level, but it can make your human life on earth very uncomfortable. It can also lead you into further suffering through other lifetimes, if you have a deep belief at some level in the karmic wheel idea. Some will decide to return and engage in a life of 'penance' because they have such a belief system, even though this may not be necessary at all.

Our belief systems, even when unconscious, must be honored. So, if one is horrible to others for an entire physical lifetime, the spirit circle may feel obligated to return again and continue the adventure from a different angle, and until this feeling of obligation is honored, that soul will not be able to pursue its path of intention. A person can get so caught up in distractions it might take a very long time to get back to the soul work.

Everything you do to harm another serves to separate you more and more from your conscious connection with Spirit. This sense of disconnection is what will make you miserable. Once you are consciously reconnected, however, the past melts away, and you can rejoin the positive flow toward love. Once you learn how to keep yourself focused and not get so distracted with all the possible destructive patterns of life, you can become more in tune with the wondrous pursuit of love knowledge, which is manifested in knowledge of the self, for we are all made of love at our core.

The search toward love is a search of our own spirit, our own soul, which is more easily accomplished if we are not distracted with a million other things. You want to be happy? Gain some focus. Look at yourself, concentrate on who you really are. Don't let all the many distractions that can tear your eyes off what you are really yearning to see emerge and take hold. But don't waste time regretting the past, for this is just another distraction, and besides, whatever you did, Spirit has already begun to turn it around to the good.

I worked through those many issues of my teen years and learned to forgive both myself and others, but it wasn't easy. Also, growing up in Hell's Kitchen has other after-effects than just the personal trauma of memories. There are constant reminders among current day activities - and herein lies the challenge. One thing is for sure - we will never outrun our past so we might as well just wrap it up in our best compassion and understanding and insight and take it with us.

One day, not so very long ago, I was particularly annoyed because my phone wouldn't stop ringing, my whole family was squabbling, my daughter was turning into a smart-mouth, Bruce was never home, my son in the navy had not called in weeks, my job was getting old, people were hounding me for psychic readings even though I wasn't doing them professionally any more, the dogs had gone crazy and ripped up my patio screen door, and I had a terrible backache. What a life! But then, later that morning my friend Patty showed up at the front door. She had come over to complain about her squabbling family and her smart-mouthed son, her husband who seemed to be always sleeping or working, her job, which was getting old, and a toothache that wouldn't leave her alone!

The two of us often laugh about how similar our lives have been from the start. We both grew up amongst alcoholism and abuse and abject poverty. We both hit the drug scene during our teen years, giving in to our surroundings. In fact, this was when we met. We became fast friends because of the way we both laughed at everything, even at our troubled families and home lives. We both married young and had children and we both left substance abuse behind us long ago, deciding to face the world sober instead. Together, we have been through more than our share of trials. We have both been what is normally referred to as 'victims' of abuse with all the associated emotional trauma.

Then there are other people. Other women and men, perfectly nice people, who have never experienced abuse, have never been subject to poverty or abandonment or severe emotional trauma. Patty and I would mention this from time to time, wondering why we would choose such a hard and lonely road for our early years instead of picking a nice and easy beginning.

"Take Mick," Patty told me once, speaking of her fun-loving husband, "his biggest gripe about his childhood is that, being the oldest, he had to get up early in the morning and make toast for his brothers because his parents would already be long gone at work."

"Oh my god," I said, "they had bread? And a *toaster*?"

Mick had a hard time living that one down but like he said, it was difficult to compete with the war stories of childhood that Patty and I had to tell.

But the heart-wrenching stories aren't the only legacy that comes out of life in Hell's Kitchen. There is also the continued dysfunction of the family unit. This is especially true in large families where there are more to tangle with, as is the case with Patty's family and mine. Somebody is always mad at somebody else. Gossip spreads like wildfire, this one and that one compete for attention, this one imagines himself God Almighty, that one can hardly drag herself out of bed. This one is continually crying about financial problems, that one is going to beat up the world, this one can't let go of the past, that one has no faith in the future, and on and on it goes until your ears are ringing, your heart is weeping, your body is tense with anger and all you want to do is fly away. You love them, you hate them, you miss their faces, you never want to see them again as long as you live.

This is the tangled web of insanity that arises out of Hell's Kitchen. This is the result of abuse, hostility, anger, irresponsibility, neglect, etc, etc. As far as I am concerned, there is no escape or salvation from Hell's Kitchen either, except through Spirit. It is our deep connection to Spirit that allows both Patty and me to 'shake it loose' and 'let it go', turning our frustrations into laughter and dissolving any leftover anger in a pool of heartfelt prayer.

Of course, the issues keep coming up. Our feelings will get hurt again, someone will lie to us, betray us, stomp on our hearts - we will always be dealing with the aftermath and casualties of Hell's Kitchen. It's not like we wake up one day and it is all just washed away, never to be remembered again. No, we will always be reminded of where we come from and of what our growing-up years were like. But living is very different when one is conscious of Spirit. The world is actually transformed! All of life is viewed with a different, more magical vision, which allows us to understand and forgive and remember the past with a new and improved insight. Growing and changing with the help of spirit guidance is what enables Patty and me to talk freely about our childhood, to laugh at it, to poke fun at some of those who harmed us, to feel gratitude for *all* the harsh lessons learned and to let go of the shame-guilt-anger combo that clung to our backsides for so many years.

But then there is the Disneyland crowd. There are some among our circle of friends who had loving, secure, cheerful, supportive childhood experiences. They grew up in nice homes with nice parents and nice siblings, ate good food and wore good quality clothes. Some were surrounded by wonderful relatives and friends as life moved along from one birthday party and Christmas delight to the next. Some of them have rich, fulfilling relationships with their grown siblings and with their aging parents. They seem very stable and secure in their relationships with their own children and spouses. Whatever their problems, they never complain about verbal abuse or emotional trauma leftover from childhood. They don't cringe when certain family members call, don't guard their bankbooks with their lives when certain relatives come to visit.

To someone from Hell's Kitchen, the Disneyland scenario can seem grossly unfair. Why did she get to sleep on a princess canopy bed when I had to sleep on an old mattress on the floor? Why did he get trips to the mountains and wrestling matches with his father while all I got was the belt buckle?

I asked Baji about it one day after an especially harrowing week dealing with my family members. Why would I choose to come into the physical realm and live in poverty, be abused and struggle with insanity all around me when I could have chosen a mansion on a hill with Ward and June Cleaver for parents? Why choose a path with so much suffering when I could just as easily have chosen joy?

Baji: *Try to imagine eternity as a concept. Year after year, decade after decade, century after century, millennia after millennia. On and on and on. Of course, you won't be here in the earth realm all the time - that would be a limiting idea! But, if you can imagine eternity even vaguely, you can see how easily beings would become bored if they didn't continuously have something interesting to do! The interests and subjects being studied right now are so vast in number and complexity they make the stars in the sky look like a mere handful of lights. Many, many diverse ideas and thoughts are being pursued, only a small number of which are now being played out in the earth realm. All sides to a given idea are explored. This means that when compassion is being studied and developed as a concept, so is cruelty and need. If one is to be supportive of another, there must be something that needs to be supported. Likewise, if there is healing, there must first be injury. All sides are delved into and looked at and experienced for the good of all.*

Some have agreed to participate in one angle, while others have agreed to participate in its opposite. So, if one has had a wonderful life and another has been through the pits of hell and back, this does not mean that one is luckier than the other, or more deserving than the other or anything like that. It simply means one has agreed to participate in a different drama this time around than someone else. Underneath it all, these two souls are a part of the same entity, which is Life and Love and All That Is.

I realize this can be very difficult to grasp at the human level, for things are split so nicely into right and wrong, good and bad, etc, because the whole world is seen as a entity consisting of opposites. Indeed, the human mind itself has been programmed to think this way, with these polarities, because this is how the physical experience is made possible. Without it, the perspective would be the same as it is in the spirit realm. But the dual nature of physical existence is an illusion created for the purpose of a unique and valuable experience. In reality, all things and all souls are connected and are at one with each other. Various aspects of this oneness are pulled apart, however, so that particular areas can be viewed and experienced in new ways.

When a spirit circle decides to embark upon a journey into the earth realm, much preparation and excitement takes place before the actual journey begins. The planning stage of this adventure is one of the most joyous times for everyone involved. Whichever part of the circle has volunteered to go into human form must choose the particular circumstances in which she or he will enter the world, as well as many of the influences that will come later on. Life-changing events are also chosen and agreed upon by participating partners. It is known that these plans are flexible and can be changed, but a particular intent is formed as the basis for the entire journey, and everything else is planned around this.

Another important thing to remember is that one particular Spirit Circle is not creating such plans in a vacuum. Other Spirit Circles as well as other spiritual entities are involved in planning processes of their own, and the intentions of these overlap and intertwine with one another. The result is an ever-expanding awareness and growth, leading to more and more creative ideas and experiences and endeavors. Creation is an ongoing process, never-ending. The whole miracle of infinity is its ability to sustain always more creativity, more growth, more enthusiasm and joy. Don't ever believe that you just came here to this world to suffer, for there is always much more to one's existence than that. You came here to learn and to teach and to further the eternal creative process. You may feel alone and abused and confused but there is a part of you, always, that knows exactly what you are doing and why.

Sometimes, this will not be understood until one has rejoined the spirit realm, but often it can be grasped while still within the human form. Pay attention to your dreams. These are one way in which you will feel the connection to your roots. You are not alone. Your experiences are never a waste, are never in vain. Whether coming from Disneyland or Hell's Kitchen, you are equally a part of Forever and of God. Appreciate it all.

Michelle Senjem and Rebecca LeTourneau

Last night the black sky did our dreaming,
and as we slept, we came to life...
as the morning who came to the night.

Michelle Senjem and Rebecca LeTourneau

Emerging From the Fog

My remaining teen years were spent in a continual tightrope walk between sobriety and intoxication as I struggled to figure out exactly what I wanted. I no longer felt urges to escape the burdens of the world through suicide but was not yet sure of what I *did* feel. The party atmosphere that constantly surrounded me did not seem as fun as it used to, or as worthwhile, and slowly but surely I distanced myself from its influence.

My parents were divorced during my teen years, as my mother finally decided she could no longer live with my father's drunken behavior, and the family kind of disintegrated into various levels of substance abuse in different directions. Many of us still got together periodically but our interests kept us separated much of the time as we all struggled to form some kind of identity for ourselves.

I found my interest in psychic phenomena and the spirit world increasing as I allowed myself longer and longer interludes of sobriety. I began to read books on the subject and started talking about things of this nature to others. Finally, I began to work at changing my apprehension into curiosity and as a consequence I began to accept myself more. There was no more need to sleep with men just to prove I was worthwhile; I was beginning to feel an acceptance from forces that lay beyond human beings.

After a time, I even started to talk to Spirit, not really knowing who I was talking to but feeling that someone was listening all the same. These were private moments and I did not share my prayer activities with others but I could tell that when I did this sort of thing my life was affected by it. Signs would come, sometimes in concrete things like a flower lying on my doorstep in the morning and other times in short visions or vivid dreams that would serve to comfort me so much I couldn't help but know that some kind of spiritual presence was with me.

As time went on and I grew older, I began to talk to Spirit about my loneliness. Even though I had many friends, I did not want to live in their world of substance abuse. It no longer attracted me as it once did. I also wanted to fall in love with someone but was afraid it might be impossible since I now had a very cynical view of men in general. I wondered if there would ever be someone who would appreciate and love me for who I was instead of just wanting to show me off on his arm.

When I was eighteen, I worked as a bartender in a small corner bar called The Rave where most of my neighborhood friends hung out. The work wasn't bad and I enjoyed talking and joking with the customers, especially since I had known many of them for years. Even though I had grown out of my desire to drink to excess, I remained a part of the party scene because this was all I had ever known and everyone I was acquainted with was a part of this lifestyle. Thankfully, no one gave me a hard time because of my sobriety habit; most of those who knew me were happy I wasn't indulging so much any more. I was no fun to be around while intoxicated. It seemed I would always see and hear things that would freak me out and someone would end up having to baby-sit me until I either passed out or sobered up. So, without any hassle, I became the sober one amongst a crowd of heavy drinkers and late-night rebels.

On my nineteenth birthday, I swung open the back door of The Rave intending to go work right away but as I walked into the dimly lit world of darts and beer I realized something was going on. A cluster of familiar faces cheered my entrance, raising glasses and beer bottles in my direction.

"It's the birthday girl!"

"Happy birthday, Michelle!"

"Happy birthday to yo-o-ou..."

I laughed, surprised at the welcome. People crowded around me, hugging, patting, squeezing, and I saw beyond them the rectangular sheet of birthday cake on the bar.

"Oh, you guys," I said, grinning widely.

84

"Hey," my friend Suzy said, laughing, "you didn't think we'd just let it go by, did you?"

"I was hoping," I teased her, only half-joking. It wasn't like I didn't appreciate the friendly intentions but I also knew it was just another excuse for everybody to get together and drink the night away. Soon, most of them wouldn't even notice if I was around or not as they lapsed deeper and deeper into a mutual oblivion. I was beginning to grow tired of the whole scene.

This is an awkward predicament for one who has grown up amidst a storm of alcohol and drug abuse because the emotional attachments are there and very deeply felt, even when the way of life itself is rejected. I was unsure of how to handle this situation so I reacted in my usual fashion with jokes, teasing and laughter. Everyone loves to laugh, drunk or sober.

I settled into work with little more disruption after the initial greetings and except for a shout or cheer directed at 'the birthday girl' now and again the night went on much the same as every other night. I mixed drinks, told jokes, and chatted with customers. A few hours later, I was busy mixing drinks when I heard someone speaking behind me.

"There is something you should probably know."

"What?"

I turned around to see who that deep voice belonged to. A tall, good-looking man with graying hair and a mischievous grin sat at the bar looking at me. I raised my eyebrows at him.

"I said," he repeated, "there is something I know that you should probably know, too."

It was clear to me that this man had been drinking for some time already so I braced myself to hear some lewd or distasteful remark.

"What's that?" I asked, holding a pleasant expression. There was no sense in upsetting the customers.

"Oh, I'll tell you, I'll tell you," he said, still grinning, "but maybe you'd better get me another beer first."

"Sure thing."

I busied myself at the tap while he looked on appreciatively.

"You're good at what you do," he said.

"Thanks."

"Still..."

I set the glass of beer in front of him and waited patiently.

"Yes?"

"Well, I would think it might be hazardous for you, working here."

I cocked my head and looked at him. An open, friendly face looked back at me. I noticed that, although his hair was gray, he looked quite young, not a whole lot older than me.

"And why would that be?" I asked, seeing that he was waiting to be prompted.

"Because you're so beautiful," he replied, matter-of-factly, "I'll bet you have to fight off the male customers with a club."

"But not you of course," I teased, intrigued by the careless air about him.

"No, not me."

"You're different from the others, are you?"

"Yep."

"Uh-huh. And what makes you so different?"

He leaned across the bar toward me, his mouth twisting at the corners into the shadows of a grin.

"What makes me so different is that I know something you don't."

"You do."

"Yep."

"Okay," I said, throwing my hands up, "I give. What is this big thing you know and I don't?"

"That I am going to marry you," he said, calmly.

I laughed out loud at this. Boy oh boy, I thought, this guy is too much!

"Listen, you," I told him, once I had recovered myself, "I wouldn't even get into an automobile with you, much less marry you so I think you had better just move along with your life, okay?"

But to my surprise he only laughed at this. He was not troubled in the least by my insult. In fact, he seemed delighted at my response and stuck out his hand, introducing himself.

"Bruce Senjem," he said.

"Michelle -"

"I know."

He smiled a big, cheery smile and left, winking and reminding me that I would be his wife someday. I just shrugged, thinking what a fool he was. Funny, though, he didn't seem bothered by the fact that I would have nothing to do with him.

He stopped by The Rave every night that week and the week after that, and the week after that. I couldn't believe this huge man with wild graying hair just would not give up the notion of marrying me, even though we had never even been on a date. Not that he wasn't trying to date me - he offered me a ride home every night but every night I refused.

"Not in this lifetime," I would say, and he would just laugh and remind me that we were going to be husband and wife before long.

"People will think you're kind of strange if you won't let your own husband drive you around once in awhile," he said.

"'Least I'll make it to where I'm going in one piece," I told him. Secretly I was thinking what a shame it was that he was always so full of alcohol by the time the bar closed because I wouldn't have minded letting him drive me home. As it was, I wasn't about to take the risk; my days of flirting with death were over.

One weekend when I finally had the night off, my friend Kim suggested I join her and her boyfriend Gary for a night on the town.

"We can go to Charlie's," she said, "they have a great band playing tonight."

Great, I thought. Just what I need - another night at a bar. But Kim said Gary had a friend he wanted me to meet - a *cute* friend, and it was Saturday night and I was bored so I went. Kim wasn't kidding about the band; they were great. And I was really impressed with Charlie's after spending so much time in the tiny, crowded bar where I worked. This place was hopping, with lots of people dancing to loud music and colored lights sweeping the room. I sighed happily, feeling all the energy around me, all the relaxation and bubbling laughter. I really should get away from work more often, I thought to myself.

Kim was right about Gary's friend, too - what a hunk! Rich Peterson was tall and blond with chiseled features and a tanned, muscular body. He was exactly the kind of man a girl dreams of standing next to in a trendy nightclub. I tried not to stare at him too much but it was hard because he looked like someone who should be famous, or at least like the cover model of some men's magazine! But when I asked him what he did for a living he said he was a baggage handler at the airport.

"God, really? I thought you were a model or something," I blurted out before I could think.

"Thanks," he said, smiling at me with those perfectly straight, white teeth. We sat at a round table, the four of us, enjoying the music along with some lighthearted conversation and as Rich inched his chair closer to mine, I decided the night was progressing along quite nicely. What a nice change from those jokers at The Rave! I realized I had been living a rather limited existence there and was preventing myself from meeting that special someone who would be perfect for me. Like Rich. I smiled at him as he said something indistinguishable, his voice drowned out by the rocking music. It didn't matter what he said anyway, I was enjoying just looking at him. After a while we danced together, moving and grooving to the joyful sounds around us before collapsing into our chairs again, our eyes shining. I accepted a second drink from Rich, who seemed to be taking it quite slowly himself, and decided it was high time I

88

started giving more of the men in the world a chance. Why was I always so picky anyway? It wasn't like there weren't any offers coming in. It seemed to me I was always finding reasons why I couldn't go out with this one or that one, choosing instead to sit at home alone or with a girlfriend, watching old movies and munching out on ice cream or popcorn. Obviously, I was missing something. Yes, it was time to change an outdated way of looking at things.

Rich reached over to grab my hand during a slow song and we danced again. I rested my head on his shoulder, feeling the starch in his white shirt and thinking how ridiculous I was to think the right man would come along and find me hiding out in my apartment. It was much more likely I would meet my destiny by getting out and mingling with the world a little more!

As we found our seats again, I began to give myself a fierce lecture while Rich and Gary fell to joking about somebody they knew. Why was I so quick to pick out flaws in men? Did I think I was so perfect? So what if Rich's hair was greased back with gel, did that make him any less of a person? Didn't men have the right to care about their appearances too? So, his nails were manicured, shouldn't this be a strong point - a *good* quality? I really had to stop picking at the gnat's eyelash here and open my mind a little. So his laugh seemed a little forced and didn't quite reach his eyes - maybe Gary just wasn't that funny. And so what if he didn't have any good stories to tell? Working at the airport probably wasn't all that interesting...

"Who is that?" Kim was yelling into my ear. I frowned, not knowing what she meant but as I turned to look where she was pointing I saw Bruce, the wild-haired guy from The Rave, sitting next to Rich. He was whispering something into his ear as my date listened intently. Then, my tall handsome hunk of a model jumped to his feet and fled. I stared in disbelief as Rick Peterson raced across the dance floor and out the door without so much as a glance back over his shoulder.

"What on earth did you say to him?" I demanded to know.

Bruce grinned, lifting his glass.

"I told him you were my girlfriend," he said, pleasantly.

"What?"

"Yeah. I explained that we had this awful fight and that you were just trying to make me jealous. But I love her, I told him. I love her so much, so could I please just talk to her for a minute?"

Speechless, I just stared at him. The audacity of this crazy man! But he was giving me that mischievous grin again, making it difficult to maintain my sense of indignation.

"Pretty decent guy," he said, clinking his glass against mine, "doesn't want to stand in the way of true love."

The image of Rich fleeing from this overgrown, wild-haired child came back to me and I couldn't help but laugh.

"You had no right to do that," I said, shaking my head at him. I was trying hard to wipe a grin off my face. Bruce leaned closer, speaking in a lower tone next to my ear and I couldn't help but notice a strange tingling deep in my stomach.

"He was too clean, wasn't he?"

"What's wrong with clean?"

"Well, I'm clean too, but he was *clean*. I mean, he was shining like china, didn't you notice? And he smelled like lavender."

I leaned back from him, determined to keep my perspective.

"He did not smell like lavender."

"Well, maybe that was the dry-cleaning fluid - did you notice he didn't have one wrinkle in his shirt? How is that possible? After sitting here this long, after dancing and running around all night - not one wrinkle! Doesn't that seem a little bit odd to you?"

I remembered the smell of starch in Rich's shirt and giggled.

"You're impossible," I said to Bruce.

"No," he replied, "I'm very possible. All you have to do is say yes."

"God. I might just have to marry you if you keep chasing all my other suitors away!"

"That's the idea," he said with a smile.

I narrowed my eyes at him.

"You must be one of those guys who gets all excited over lost causes," I said. "Even when you don't have a chance in hell you don't give up. Kind of like a lab rat in a treadmill, thinking it will get to that cheese on a string someday."

Again, my teasing insults only made Bruce laugh. We couldn't help but make each other laugh - it came so naturally to both of us. So, instead of enjoying my date with the beautiful Rich Peterson, I found myself spending the rest of the evening with this crazy, soft-spoken man who drank too much and shook off my insults with hearty laughter. What else could I do but marry him?

Slowly but surely, the burdened feelings of my past began to lift from my shoulders as Bruce and I began our new life together. We bought a house and set about carving out a future for ourselves. He obviously loved me, which was a wonderful feeling, and I also experienced a great sense of relief at being pulled out of the party scene to which I had been accustomed. Bruce still drank too much from time to time. But I no longer felt obligated to attend the latest party or late-night bash because I was a married woman now. And when our first child was born, I knew I was free from that old life forever.

When our beautiful boy came into this world, I knew immediately that we had met before. His curly blond hair and blue eyes were a joy to behold but it was his sweet nature that I recognized. Right from the start he felt more familiar to me than anything ever had before and he responded to me as if he, too, recognized our deep, soul-level connection. When I named him Christopher, he smiled at me as if to say yes, that's it. Others insisted it wasn't really a smile - his face just happened to contort that way as he shifted uncomfortably with gas - but I knew better. Christopher and I understood each other.

Three short years later, his sister Jillian came into our lives. Another beautiful baby, this time with dark hair and an intense gaze, she exhibited a strong will from the very first day. Again, I was amazed at the way she seemed to recognize me right away, and I her. My belief in past lives and soul connections became much more solid after the birth of my children because what I felt while looking into their knowing eyes filled me with wonder and a sense of certainty I had never felt before.

When I look back to those years I can see the steps that led me through my awakening to life. It started with the birth of my children because they created a firm resolve in me to remain forever separated from the substance abuse patterns that had plagued most of the people around me all my life. Also, during this time a close friend of mine lost her thirteen-year-old son in a tragic accident that involved a drunk driver. This shook me to my core, watching what she was going through, wondering why on earth any God would take such a young boy away from his loving mother. This tragedy, coupled with the death of my father a few years later, sent me headlong down a path of fervent questioning. I was desperate to know about death and what it meant. Instead of ignoring the twinges and whisperings from Spirit, I deliberately tuned in, trying to decipher the meanings and reasons for these occurrences. My intense longing to know the answers overshadowed the fear that had plagued me most of my life and I stopped trying to hide from what I knew was real.

Bit by bit, the veil was lifted from my eyes and I began to see for the first time what it meant to actually commune with Spirit, to realize there really is more to our existence than we might think. Through trial and error, I learned how to detect what my intuition was telling me. I learned to listen to the whisperings in my ears until I could finally make sense of what I was hearing. I began to pay attention to all the many signs and coincidences and warnings and clues surrounding me each day, and to put these things to good use. The result was a life transformed.

The funny thing is, it wasn't even all that hard. Once I opened my mind and heart, allowing myself to become inquisitive, Spirit responded quickly, and with joy. Feelings of love and warmth and complete acceptance swept over me time and again, filling my being with a sense of bliss never before experienced. It became apparent, almost immediately, that there was another presence around me, an invisible force emanating pure love. All I had to do was tune in and there it was. Making myself sit quietly, relaxing my muscles and giving my full attention to Spirit resulted in meaningful dialog with spirit entities, and these conversations changed my entire way of thinking. The world had not changed but I had - and consequently, I *saw* an entirely new world. No matter what happened, whether good or bad, it affected me differently than it would have before because *I* was different. Experience after experience served to strengthen my new way of thinking until beliefs were set solidly in place and I no longer doubted what I knew to be true.

This is when my life truly began. This is when I began to finally pursue the path that would set me in alignment with my spiritual purpose. My spirit connections became foremost in my mind and focus, leading me to venture down paths much different from those I had been used to before. Now, I was relying on spiritual guidance and direction. I no longer felt alone or unimportant, for there was a permanent circle of friends around me at all times. My actions and adventures were no longer just for me - they reflected the interests and input of the others within my Spirit Circle as well. I no longer had to rely on just myself to provide insights or explanations; I had access to a much wider scope of vision as seen from the spirit realm!

Embracing the so-called 'psychic' aspects of my nature, instead of trying to deny them, drastically altered my way of thinking and responding to just about everything. It's too bad the concept of 'psychics' has gained such a questionable reputation in the world because it limits the acceptance of many great treasures lying within us. Everyone is psychic, or can be. It is a natural part of the human experience if we would only remember to pay attention. What we focus on is what will become more and more developed over time. I happen to be very interested in the workings of spirit so I focus on these kinds of issues all the time. Not everyone will have such an intense interest in spirit work but all *can* if they choose.

For me, the adventures of this physical lifetime have led me into situations where my psychic talents are constantly being developed. This is not to say I still don't have much to learn because I do and always will. This is the great and joyous fun of eternity. There is no grand stepping off place where we are all done forevermore and just sit around shining like the sun - although we *could* if we wanted to. Eternity is not a linear destination; rather it is a circular existence, ongoing and everlasting, one adventure after another, exactly as we wish it, plan it, create it, and live it.

Mija: It is so wonderful to watch those in the human realm as they experience physical life! All the many things they encounter, all the adventures and joys and sorrows and fears and discoveries - it is like no other existence! Falling in love is an incredibly fun adventure, both to participate in and to observe, and Michelle's experience with Bruce is no exception.

She did not realize it at the time, how could she? But it was very important for their future relationship that he pursue her as determinedly as he did. Bruce was to put our Michelle through many years of trial with his periodic drinking and long stretches away from home as he drove trucks across the country. There were a few times Spirit needed to intervene in order to keep her with him, although she was always free to leave him if she wished. But the way he went about winning her in the first place was to forever remain a fond memory for her and helped her to maintain affection for him even after he put her through the wringer. Of course, there was also the fact that he did love her in a way that transcended her beauty - a fact she forced him to prove by putting on a great many pounds! He was able to see through this and loved her spirit, her soul essence, which was so pure and loving, and Michelle could sense this even though his actions confused her so often.

Michelle also planned to be married young and have her children early in life for good reason. She was in a state to mother at that time in a most intense way and she thoroughly enjoyed those years with her young children. She also knew she would have some very intense work later in life that would have made it more difficult to concentrate on young children then, so she embraced motherhood when it would be most convenient for her to do so. Oh, the fun she had! Not that she didn't have heart-wrenching terrors too, for she did. Raising children is always hard on the heart; this is the nature of parenting! But the joys outweighed the hardships and Michelle was filled with happiness when with her babies. They spent joyous time together, playing and laughing and loving, discovering the world and new life through each other's eyes.

However one's young life goes, it will prepare that person for later life and will help determine how they love, who they love and what kind of family ties they form. It was good for Michelle to be alone so much with her children when they were so young, even though she often missed Bruce, because she formed such a close bond with them and learned a great deal through focusing her attention on their development. Those years were growing years, shaping and forming Michelle's thoughts and beliefs for her later life. Many of us in her Spirit Circle spent our time in great amusement and joy as we watched over them and observed the way they interacted with one another. Of course things were not always fuzzy and warm - a young mother with two energetic children! But even the squabbles and the misunderstandings and the anxieties that arose were intriguing to those of us watching from the spirit realm; we cherished every bit, and still do. I still like to go back and watch Michelle engage in a power struggle with Jillian, who is one of the most determined souls on the planet! The way they danced their mother-daughter dance when Jill was very little is a joy to behold. Each knew the other was a mighty intuitive being, and each was sure she could sway the other into thinking something different anyway!

Whatever moments parents have with children, however brief, is a precious and lovely treasure that exists for eternity. These moments can and will be visited over and over again, as many times as is desired. Just because these times are but memories to humans, they are available to us now, and will be to you when you have rejoined your spirit families. They can also be available to those humans who have mastered the art of astral and time travel; something I have a feeling Michelle will continuously be engaging in during her later years.

Bruce was a high point in our Michelle's life when he appeared in the plans of her heart and soul, and this is as it was meant to be, for she wanted to hang on through those rough years, knowing things would greatly improve if she did. Of course, she wasn't consciously aware of this knowledge while it was going on, but we knew. And, sure enough, she hung in there and Bruce stopped drinking and stopped driving for a living. He came back home and began to participate fully in family life again, although his tendency to work incessantly is always with him. Michelle was able to fall in love with him again, remembering how it used to be in the beginning, and was able to let go of those bad times. She was able to do this because of her constant work over the years to bring herself in alignment with her higher self and her Spirit Circle. She is never out of contact with us for long, and so we are able to help her much more than we could otherwise!

It's true that Bruce was driving truck for many years and was away from home a lot, leaving me alone with two small children. At first, his absences only made our love for one another stronger, prolonging our honeymoon period for quite some time since we always missed each other so much. I also thoroughly enjoyed my time with the children; seeing the world through their unbiased gaze was a profound learning experience for me. My love for life grew and grew as I discovered the joys of living in the spontaneous emotions of the moment. But as the years went by and the stresses of family life increased, I began to resent Bruce's absences. I started to wonder how he could spend so much time away from us when he was supposed to love us so much! There were times when I almost left him, it is true. And, as I look back I can see the little nudges of Spirit that helped me decide to stay just a bit longer. Being told by a famous psychic that he was going to die soon, dreams that made me worry about his health, the attachment he had to the kids, along with other things served to make me hesitate long enough for things to get better.

When Bruce finally did give up his over-the-road career and took a job in town, it was a major adjustment for both of us. I was used to being independent and making the daily decisions of life completely on my own so was not at all thrilled to hear his opinion about certain things. Also, he was not used to the day-to-day grind and sacrifices of family life on such a regular basis, so would take to burying himself in work just to keep himself out of the picture for a few more hours. It took time but gradually we became used to being around one another again and life became much easier. I liked having him near and he learned to calm down once he realized that life with children is naturally chaotic and getting all upset about it won't change a thing.

Later, I understood how much I was forced to learn because of Bruce's absences during the early years of our marriage. Without him gone, I would never have developed such an independent nature so quickly. It would have been too easy to lean on him, letting him make all the decisions and just drift along like an agreeable shadow. As it was, I had to learn to be self-sufficient in many ways. Shoveling the sidewalk, fixing leaky pipes, changing fuses, fiddling with the car engine; all the things I was thrown into doing because Bruce wasn't around, helped me to gain a sense of myself and my abilities I may not have discovered otherwise, or at least not until much later in life. Even though I was not too happy about these things at the time, I can now see how they were good for my development and helpful to me in the following years.

Mija: It's interesting and significant that Michelle's children are what really drew her out of her past way of thinking. She was not totally intent upon continuing her physical life here on this planet until they came along. Even though she had not tried to take her own life for many years, her motivation for living had not really blossomed yet and before her babies came she was just kind of drifting along without passion or direction. But once the children came, she was transformed. This is another reason why it was necessary for her to have children when she did. Otherwise, her awakenings could have taken much, much longer.

Much of the repressed interest Michelle had in the spiritual realm really emerged after her children were born. She was amazed by them so much, her attention turned toward spiritual things and psychic phenomena - especially because she felt so strongly that she had known them both before. Because of her past history of fear relating to extrasensory perception and spirit contact, it was easier for Michelle to focus on these things in her children than in herself. She worked with them, or I should say she played with them, to develop their own psychic and intuitive abilities, taking great care to keep from stifling any interests they might have.

Through their easy acceptance of their own inner selves and intuitive natures, Chris and Jill served to create a healing effect in Michelle as her own childhood terrors began to give way to enlightenment. As she watched the miracle of uninhibited children progressing through life, Michelle was able to shed many inhibitions of her own. She could finally see that a natural trust and joy in spirit was not impossible. Her faith and trust in Spirit was enhanced and she was able to become more and more in tune with her own inner being as her children grew and reflected this spiritual presence and psychic ability back to her.

I can clearly remember how amazed I was, over and over again, as little Chris demonstrated an intuitive knowing that was almost startling. It came so naturally to him! I remembered a time, long ago when I had experienced similar premonitions but had been so frightened of them! It had taken me years to accept the fact that these visions and insights were not a horrible curse but a blessing. Even now, I had to remind myself not to be afraid when I went into a trance state or when I would get a flash of something from someone else's mind. It was wonderful to see my son relate so easily to his natural abilities, totally unconcerned with the opinions of others. I became determined that he would not experience the alienation from himself that I had gone through. He would not be taught to doubt the invisible world, the spirit world. He would not be told that it was all his imagination. No, I would help him develop this ability that came so naturally to him and I would teach him that it was a wonderful gift, a blessing given to all humans. He was not odd or strangely different from everyone else but was incredible and special in his own way. He was totally accepted by the spirit world, by all of life - just the way he was. Whatever he felt to be true was something to be honored and respected. This is what I would teach my child. I would tell him to trust his own instincts, to listen to the whisperings in his ears and to the sensations in his physical body.

Chris kept me in a constant state of delight. We played our games, visited with friends, and shared our insights and dreams with one another. Even at the tender age of three, he was interested in his dreams and would wake up with magical stories to tell. I would listen, amused and enthralled, as I prepared breakfast for the two of us.

Chris was three years old when Jill came into our lives. She also amazed me from the beginning, just as her brother did, although she was quite different from him in temperament. Chris was immediately taken with her and decided right away that she needed his unique style of protection. If she was in the living room swinging in her baby swing he would play nearby, stopping whatever he was doing every so often to listen to and feel what was going on in the surrounding atmosphere. If she was in her crib sleeping, he would tiptoe in there looking around the room in that same intent manner to make sure she was in a safe place. Before I ventured out the front door with Jill, he would poke his head outside and look around, sniffing the air and listening like a funny little wolf-boy. Then, if all was well, he would step through the door and wave me forward.

These little acts of protection amused me to no end because I always felt that Jill was completely safe. Once, though, when Chris made me wait indoors for a few moments, a navy blue Chevy without a muffler roared past at high speed, its deafening sound permeating the neighborhood. Since we would have been on the sidewalk the car wouldn't have harmed us but the noise would probably have startled Jill and made her cry. So, even this little event made me believe in the power of my son's intuition.

Jill, also from a very early age, showed signs of a strongly developed intuitive sense. An extremely willful child, she had the ability to size up a situation in a matter of seconds and could easily manipulate her surroundings in order to create what she wanted. It took the rest of us some time to learn how to stand up to her; we were so taken aback by the force of her convictions. She was not a defiant toddler but had a unique sense of self and an absolute belief in her own abilities. Many times, I would find myself debating some small issue with her only to find out that she had been right the whole time, seeing the situation much clearer than I did. This can be pretty disconcerting when you are staring incredulously into the innocent-wise face of a two-year-old!

"No," she announced, matter-of-factly, when I suggested she take off her shoes and socks to play in the sandbox.

"But you'll get your shoes full of sand," I told her.

"Soos *on*."

"Jill, look at that little girl over there. She's barefoot. See how much fun she's having?"

"No," she replied, climbing into the sandbox.

I sighed, thinking about how dirty her white socks were going to get. But Jill was smiling at me already as she ran her hands lightly across the top of the sand. I smiled back, resignedly. Socks could be washed.

"Why don't you use your pail?" I asked her. "Fill it up like this."

I dug my hands into the sand, scooping up a pile to throw in her pail. Jill frowned at me, shaking her head.

"Don't," she said.

"Fine, fine."

I sat back on the grass, watching the other kids play. They were all barefoot, all scooping up sand with their hands and throwing it into their pails while Jill continued to sit quite still, running her hands cautiously back and forth around her.

All at once, a scream broke out. The little girl I had been pointing out to Jill earlier was crying and screaming as she held up a bloody hand for her mother to see.

"Oh, my goodness," her mother exclaimed, snatching her daughter out of the sand. I rushed forward as well, looking to see what had caused the injury. There, in the sand, just a few feet from where Jill was sitting, was a large piece of broken glass. The little girl was not cut badly but it looked terrible because the little cut on her finger was bleeding profusely. All the other children quickly hopped out of the sandbox as mothers came running from every direction. I grabbed Jill, too, but she resisted.

"All gone," she protested.

I stared at her.

"Gone? How do you know? There could be more glass in there, Jilly."

She just looked at me as if I were the dumbest soul on the planet.

"Well, let me just make sure," I said, somewhat chagrined. I dug around in the sand for a while, but there appeared to be no more cut glass anywhere in the vicinity. When I turned back around to look at my daughter, she had removed her shoes and socks and was plunging her hands into the sand without reserve.

"I wouldn't trust that sandbox," one of the other mothers told me as she whisked her son away. But I was beginning to realize that Jill had sensed what I had not - that something dangerous was lurking near - so she had been very careful in the beginning, not sure exactly where the danger was. But after the little girl was cut and the piece of glass was revealed, Jill knew that the danger was past and she was free to play uninhibited. Of course, she was far too young to articulate all of this to me so she reacted in her usual obstinate way. Only, instead of seeing her as stubborn and uncooperative, I then realized she was merely following her own intuition. She was very much attached to her own senses and believed totally in what they told her.

After a few incidents like that one, I began to trust and honor Jill's opinions more and more. For all I knew, she could have spirits whispering in her own ears like I had when I was her age. Who was I to doubt such a thing? I knew better. Thus, through both of my children, I learned to appreciate the assistance of invisible forces as never before. I was not the only one taking care of my two beautiful babies - there were many helpers around us!

Who Am I

I am not so old
or faint of heart,
or with a hat
on my head I am
not so dignified
or warmly understood.

The air breaks over the
mountain's breath,
the cliffs have their eyes
on a blue sky
and from up top the
higher ground from where
the mountain sees,
the old river, the ocean
not so young,
the forest alone
but with brilliant eyes,
looking toward some
distant place.

— Mike East

Past Lives: Do They Matter?

He stood over me, a fierce frown on his rough, round face, and waved his arms back and forth over his head.

"Too much," he yelled, "too much!"

"Too much what?" I asked, recoiling with fright. This sturdy man in front of me, not tall but broad and powerful, looked terribly angry and menacing standing there. Where were we? Somewhere dark, it seemed, and damp. I felt myself backing away from this fierce stranger. His hair, black as the midnight sky, was cut short over his strong Asian features. I did not recognize him at all, but felt he did not like me.

"You," he thundered, thrusting an accusing finger toward me, "too much!"

I didn't understand. What had I done to make this man so angry? Again, I took a few steps backward but this time I felt someone behind me. A startled scream escaped from my lips as I whirled around to find myself facing *him* again!

"What, what," I cried, covering my face with my hands, "too much what?"

Suddenly, I felt myself being lifted up, up, up through the damp, dark ceiling into the black sky, up, up, up until my heart lurched with terror and I woke up.

"Worry," I said aloud. I was sitting straight up in bed, my heart pounding. Blinking, I turned my head this way and that, peering into the dim light of my bedroom. What a dream! Who was that crazy character? Some angry Chinese man yelling at me. I must have had another nightmare. Don't be alarmed, I told myself firmly; he is just a figment of your imagination. You must be angry with yourself about something.

Too much, too much, he had said over and over. Too much what? But then, it dawned on me that I had spoken a word upon waking. Worry. Too much worry. Aha, I thought, I am worrying too much again. With a sigh of relief, I settled back against the

105

pillows and thought about this. Obviously, I was sending myself a message. It was true I had been spending too much time in worry again. Being a wife and mother of two growing children, it was hard not to. I felt Bruce was working himself too hard and was not appreciated by his superiors. I didn't want him to get so stressed out he ended up having a heart attack! And the kids were getting so independent, so daring and reckless. Chris had been riding down a ski slope on his mountain bike just the week before! And Jill had been hanging out with a new group of kids who seemed to hate school and adults and rules of any kind. They also appeared to despise color since they only wore black.

Silently, I called on Baji for help. I knew it did no good to worry so much, but I felt I just couldn't help myself. What I heard as I drifted off to sleep again, was that worry could teach me things, too, and that I would stop fretting so much when I *chose* to stop.

Two days later, I was preparing a pot roast for dinner when my cousin Mary called from California. I hadn't heard from her in months and was happy to hear her voice.

"How are you?" I asked, glad to sit down for a bit and take a break.

"I'm freaking out," she said, excitedly. "There is a Chinese spirit sitting here on my living room rug and he wants to talk to you!"

"*What?*"

I was shocked because, for one thing, Mary was not one to talk about psychic experiences and for another, she happened to mention a *Chinese* spirit. She was nervous but adamant about relaying this experience to me - as it was happening. She said his arms were crossed over his chest and he looked very angry. Immediately, my dream of the other night came to mind. Who was this spirit and why was he so upset with me?

"He says he... knows you," Mary said, "and that he is... ah... one of your ancestors."

"Really?"

"Yeah ... um ... okay, wait a minute."

Mary became silent for a moment while I drew a deep breath to calm myself. My hands were trembling as I thought about being contacted from a long-ago ancestor.

"His name is Ging," Mary said, speaking rapidly now. "He is a Mongolian warrior. He has killed many, many men while in fierce combat. He is strong and fearless..." she paused for a moment, then her voice rose higher as she went on, "...wait, um... he is saying that he is... Michelle?"

"Yes, I'm here."

"No, he's saying *he* is Michelle. He is you!"

"Oh my —"

"Are you Mongolian?"

"We have some Mongolian in us from my dad's side," I said, my voice filled with wonder. "What does he want to tell me?"

"Oh...oh —" Mary exclaimed, "he's gone!"

"No," I protested, "he can't be. Look again."

But Ging had vanished, leaving me hanging once again. Frustrated, but extremely excited, I blurted out the story of my dream to Mary, who was fascinated.

"I thought he was just a figment of my imagination," I said.

"Michelle, this is weird. Stuff like this never happens to me. I was just sitting here reading when all of a sudden I started thinking about you. Then, I looked over and there he was. I almost jumped right out of my skin! And all he kept saying was to call Michelle, call Michelle. So, I did."

"What did he look like?"

"Well, he was a little bit hazy, you know, kind of ghost-like, but part of the time I could see him clearly. He's kind of short but really muscular and his face is kind of scarred up —"

"Yes, yes," I exclaimed, "that's him!"

Mary and I went on talking for another two hours that day, our mutual excitement growing ever higher and more intense as we recounted those strange visits from Ging over and over. That night I tried to dream about him again but remembered nothing.

The next night brought the same disappointment. I knew I was being silly; Ging would obviously come to me when he was good and ready. I shouldn't try to force things, I thought. But I was so impatient and excited about the whole thing, I wanted to know more. Then, a few days later, Mary called to say he had visited her again. This time she had been lying on the sofa, just waking up from a nap, when suddenly he was sitting on her chest! She couldn't really see him this time but was just able to catch the sight of a sort of 'blob' of energy. However, she could definitely feel the weight of him crushing off her air supply.

"I thought I was going to choke to death," she said, "it was scary."

"Did he say anything?"

"Just one thing over and over: 'this is what fear does. This is what fear does. This is what fear does.'"

"Hmm."

I sat very still, thinking. Why was this Ging visiting Mary instead of me? She wasn't even related to him, coming from my mother's side of the family, so why was he contacting me through her?

"Are you afraid of something?" she wanted to know.

"My son wants to jump out of an airplane and my daughter is turning into a vampire," I said, dryly, "you bet I'm afraid."

"Maybe he's telling you not to be," Mary suggested. "Maybe he is protecting them."

"I think he wants me to know I don't have to be afraid of *him*," I said, surprising myself. Where had that come from? I hadn't thought it before I said it - the words just came out. But I was sure that was it. Ging was contacting me through Mary because he knew how much his presence frightened me. And obviously he was aware of the relationship I had with my cousin, which was one of mutual respect and admiration, so he revealed himself to her in order to send me a message without scaring me to death!

That night, and for many nights after that, I took some time to talk to Ging before falling asleep. I told him I would try very hard not to fear him if he visited me again. I affirmed my trust in his intentions because I felt they were honorable. And, sure enough, Ging began to emerge in my dreams again before too long. His manner had not changed; he continued to appear with that same fierce, angry demeanor, but I was able to look beyond all that and see the kindness in his eyes.

His messages were always about strength and courage and the intensification of focus and he usually appeared to me when I was becoming too distracted with anxiety or getting discouraged about various aspects of my life.

I came to realize over time that much of the reason he frightened me was due to the harsh symbolism he sometimes used in order to get a point across. Severed heads and small bodies frozen in snow may have seemed tame to him but these images really shook me up. He has since toned down his use of such morbid symbolism as he understands my strong aversion to it but he still has a way of coming at me full force, startling me out of my socks in order to drive his message home.

I do not speak to Ging often, the way I do with Baji, and his presence is not so apparent in my conscious life. Baji has informed me, however, that Ging represents one of my 'other lives' and is a part of our Spirit Circle. I have not had any memory flashes of this warrior life but Baji says it is not necessary for me to experience this in my current life - and that I really wouldn't want to remember anyway!

Another past-life spirit named Marcus revealed himself to me in some recurring dreams some years later, but again, his influence was explained to me more by Baji than anyone else. Apparently we, as a Spirit Circle, have lived numerous lives through Marcus who has been manifested as a teacher, monk, and as a scientist many times. Baji says I have received many aspects of Marcus' nature, including my intense love for animals and my interest in the natural world. He has spent many lives immersed in a study of the physical world so when I find myself becoming absorbed in learning about a particular plant, flower, tree or animal, I know this is Marcus' interest coming through.

Also, as a monk he studied many different religions, which is why I had no real need for this in my current life. Growing up in an environment where no religious beliefs were held made me feel a bit out of place in the world at times, especially when I was young. But, in fact, I have already been in most of those places, participating in traditional beliefs and religions, so now I am free to pursue other avenues, thanks in large part to Marcus and his experiences of the past.

I have felt the presence of other beings who also seem to be scientists of some kind. I never see them clearly but there appear to be a lot of them and they all seem very smart, with much greater knowledge than I have. But these clustered beings are not so terribly serious like Marcus is. Often, I can hear them giggling and making fun of me, especially if I am getting too self-important or judgmental. They also seem to find humor in the many distractions I find myself engaged in. Once, when some friends and I drove to a casino several miles away, these scientist beings sprung forth to form a tight group around me the minute I walked through the door of that place!

"Oh boy," I could hear them saying, "here we go. What is she doing now?"

Then they proceeded to fire off in rapid succession the grim statistics about my chances of winning. It didn't matter what machine I sat down at or where I went in the casino, they would immediately begin to sputter out the mathematical odds of each endeavor, laughing and laughing at my belief that I might actually win something. I lost over a hundred dollars before I finally stopped trying to ignore them and even my annoyance at having to admit they were right gave them a chuckle!

Baji: Michelle's keen interest in her past lives has led her to meet several of her former selves and from time to time she has

110

needed to be reminded that her point of focus would be better placed in the NOW. However, some knowledge of past life experiences can be helpful to humans during their current lifetimes if they apply this knowledge in a useful way. Always, the goal is to better understand the inner workings of the Self.

Each member of our Spirit Circle has existed on the human plane at one time or another - and Michelle was with us then as we are with her now. We remain, always, a group entity. As a group consciousness, we learn not only from the physical plane through our human manifestation (Michelle), but also from many surrounding dimensions as well.

One benefit of some measure of past life recall is its ability to awaken a recognition of one's strength and courage. As humans you have been through much more than you realize. There are depths to your being you haven't even begun to fathom as yet. Remembering certain instances from your past lives can sometimes awaken these talents and capabilities within you, fueling your creative powers.

One of the greatest challenges I have faced is within the lesson of enjoying life freely rather than succumbing to it with a mindset of obligation. So many times I held back from doing things I really wanted to do or from saying things I really wanted to say because I was afraid of how it might look or because I was worried about offending people. Over the years of working with Spirit I have been able to distance myself from this rigid way of being, although this physical world has never been easy for those who stand firmly rooted within the authenticity of their own nature. If a person sticks out in a crowd, he or she is often viewed as crazy or dangerous or some combination of the two.

I am neither crazy nor dangerous but it took me a long time to shed my fear of being thought of this way. One very significant revelation helped me a great deal in this regard, and it happened when I met Maricell.

Maricell was me, I was her, and we lived in England many centuries ago. I remember walking down through the Piccadilly with my friend the bobby, eager to meet up with my artist friends. They were a flamboyant bunch, full of laughter and raucous jokes, their view of the world always a bit tainted with ridicule. These people had very little structure in their lives and very little money but I was greatly moved by their booming lust for life, regardless of the hardships they faced.

I know I wasn't anything like these people and perhaps they accepted my presence partly because of the monetary assistance I gave them but I feel there was a warmth between us and a genuine respect, even though they often teased me and laughed at me because of my station in life. I am very certain of the fact that my heart cried out for the freedoms they enjoyed, for my own circumstances did not permit such things. Even my time with these artists was covert; I had to hide and pretend in order to be with them.

One of the strongest memories I have of this life is the way I felt inside then. Surrounded by beautiful things and by wealthy, powerful people, I was screaming silently in my mind much of the time. The wealthy family I was a part of had some kind of public position so we were on continual display. I had to be extremely careful of everything I did or said to make sure I did not disgrace the family name.

I know I did not feel very much for the people around me, realizing how little they needed my input, and I dreamed of breaking free from my societal chains to run free with my crazy artist friends. I am quite sure I never broke free in that life. It was a world where I sat very straight in chairs, holding my entire body in a rigid posture at all times. There was so much stuffy clothing to wear, I felt suffocated all the time. And the pressure of maintaining a good name was not simply a family obligation, it carried with it real and terrible threats which frightened me a good deal. A wrong image or displaced remark could get people killed back then, especially people in power, and we all knew it.

Memories of this life as Maricell have come back to me many times, and I can see this life more clearly than any of the others. I can also see Maricell quite clearly at times. She is tall and quiet with deliberate movements, soft speech, and a regal air about her. It was always her form I was tuned into when I was hesitant to take risks or to reveal various parts of myself to others. Together, we have communicated our way through many issues dealing with fear, and she is ecstatic when I take the rebel aspects of our nature to new levels. Maricell has been one of my strongest inspirations to develop my intuitive skills because she sees it as liberation from the lonely life she endured for all our sakes.

These days, Maricell's assistance comes to me most when I am feeling unsure of myself in new situations. Her influence is a calming one and when I hear her wise, soothing voice in my head or around my ears, I am filled with an instant confidence. In her restricted life, Mary was exposed to many areas of life I have not experienced. She understands the intricate web of power and money and, although these things disgusted her at the time, she is eager to provide me with various insights, which greatly help me in my current life. She is also most helpful when I meet someone who seems very polished and talks very smoothly and I am not sure about the level of sincerity behind the words being spoken. Since Maricell spent countless hours listening to the drivel of politicians and successful businessmen, she is quickly able to discern intent. I count heavily on her keen observational skills whenever I am dealing with someone whose intentions I question.

I don't spend so much time exploring past-life adventures now as I used to but these memory lessons continue to emerge every now and again as I make my way through current situations. I am very comforted by the knowledge that these beings of my Spirit Circle are always near, guiding, observing, reminding. I am grateful to have past life experiences to draw on when facing challenges in my current drama because recalling these bits and pieces often has a very enlightening effect on my present life. Remembering certain things can wake you up to certain patterns that seem to keep resurfacing and can help you understand yourself better. Everyone will experience such past life memories differently, depending on their present needs. For me, the information comes through dreams and visions, often in a very brief but intense way, and leaves me with some kind of profound insight to my nature.

One example of this happened to me while suffering from severe back pain. I was lying on the sofa feeling a bit drowsy and wondering why I was creating so much pain for myself. As is my habit, I asked for guidance right away because I knew Spirit could tell me what I needed to know if only I was open enough to hear it.

As I lay there, my eyes slowly closed, and when they did I was unable to open them again. It was as if there were a heavy weight pressed against my eyelids, holding them in place. The shock of this was immediately followed by the recognition that I was seeing a vision inside my head. I was looking up at the faces of two men - soldiers in gray uniforms - who were snarling at me in a hateful manner. Then, suddenly I was out of my body looking down at myself as the two soldiers beat me with all of their might. I saw then that I was a man, also a soldier, but my uniform was blue.

I knew the men wanted me to tell them something; they insisted I give them the information I knew I could not give. Finally, when they saw I was not going to speak even in my bloody state, they gave up. Only they didn't let me go. Instead, they dropped a very large and heavy boulder onto my lower back, crushing my body against the ground. They left me there to die, bleeding inside and out, alone and frightened.

This vision, which lasted only a few moments, left as quickly as it came and I was able to open my eyes again. By then I was so startled and excited, I was no longer tired, and called on those in my Spirit Circle to come forward and explain the vision to me. I knew it had something to do with my back; I could still feel the pain from that boulder! I forced myself to quiet down my thoughts and relax so Baji could come to me. I pictured his face in my mind, his wise, kind eyes gazing at me with that loving expression that was always such a comfort. I was surprised, then, when he came to me by way of a female voice whispering into my left ear.

"Aha," she said, "you have injured your back again in the very same place - what does this tell you?"

I told her I didn't know; I needed her help.

"You are again holding in the truth that can set you free, Michelle," Mija whispered.

"What truth?" I asked, but even as I asked, I knew. My family, my siblings - so many in my life were caught up in destructive patterns, struggling with alcohol and drug abuse, mired in financial difficulties, constantly caught up in unhealthy relationships. And I was always getting myself involved, getting caught up in their chaos, continually striving to make their lives easier, *bending over backwards* to protect them from themselves.

The message came through loud and clear, stunning me because I had not been thinking consciously of these things at all. I had to stop holding in my feelings. I needed to tell my family members how I felt about their destructive behavior, whether this caused a rift between us or not.

I decided I would not hold in the truth any longer; I would speak it out loud. I did not want another broken back! But I wondered about that past life situation and about the brutal ending of that physical adventure. I asked Mija if I should have given those two soldiers the information they wanted.

"Not necessarily," she said, "because you were willing then to accept the consequences of not speaking. However, in your current life situation you may not be so willing to accept such a consequence. The important thing is for you to understand that this back injury *is* the consequence of your denial to speak the truth, of your refusal to tell what you know. Your unconscious yearning for the truth is so strong it is injurious to you to keep silent."

I was amazed that such a thing as holding my tongue could cause me so much physical pain, yet I recognized the truth of Mija's words. After that, I began to speak up more and more to those in my family who were constantly creating their own problems. It was difficult, but I managed to get the truth out in bits and pieces, as my courage allowed.

This remains an issue with me, although it is becoming easier and easier for me to speak my mind. Often, our most difficult transformations are those we must make in our relationships with family members. But I know now how harmful it can be to swallow the words of truth instead of allowing them to come out. When we deny ourselves, putting up a false front, we are helping no one. In the end, speaking our truth is the most loving thing we can do for anybody.

I believe most of us have lived many, many lifetimes, and that we have memory flashes now and again whether we realize them for what they are or not. Sometimes, a place you see on television or read about may feel very familiar to you even though you have never been there. You might get a hazy recollection of someone's face or voice which is not from this life and yet feels as dear to you as those of your present-day family!

Of course, the past life memories do not provide me with many details; they are but flashes of memory visiting me. But I will often be brought back to a previous life in order to face something in it time and again. Thus, some past life situations become clearer than others over time. But I always recognize myself and come away with some type of insight to my current situation.

Baji: Every human being is affected and influenced by their past lives, whether they realize it or not. Sometimes these influences will be revealed in the form of phobias, such as an illogical fear of water or heights even though one has never had a bad experience with such a thing in their current life. Other times, these influences are manifested in the form of a particular personality trait or certain behaviors, or by way of a unique gift such as a powerful singing voice or a genius capacity for mathematics. It is true that these things are carried in the genes, but even genes are affected by past experiences and lifetimes. This does not take anything away from one's individuality, for all are a part of a group consciousness, which is then divided into distinct individual personalities for the purpose of engaging in the earthly adventure. While in the spirit realm, these individual personalities persist but can also be dissolved into a group entity when this is desired. There are situations and interests for both ways of being - individual and at-one-ment.

It is also true that interest in past lives is not always beneficial for those doing the searching, especially if it distracts them too much from focusing on their current life. Always, the point of power is in the NOW. One can spend entirely too much energy traveling back to other places and time frames while neglecting their current path. The only reason a human would benefit from past life knowledge is to further their understanding of Self so that they can manifest more creative energy NOW. Thus, when various aspects of a Spirit Circle are revealed, a person comes to know those parts of him or herself they did not know before.

For instance, Michelle had no urge to think of herself in terms of a fierce warrior with rough and intense mannerisms until she met Ging. After she came to know him, however, she was better able to make use of his energy in her current life. This came in handy many times, especially when she was dealing with a fearful situation or learning to install boundaries around her that guarded against those who would suck her dry with their neediness.

It is possible to get to know those in one's Spirit Circle without delving into past life experiences but sometimes these *memories can illustrate the nature of someone in a very meaningful and astounding way. If something by way of a past life experience reveals itself through a dream or vision or clear memory, it should be used in the way it is intended - to further one's creative powers and abilities in **this** life.*

A human is always free to spend his or her entire lifetime here on earth engrossed in past life memories but this will only serve to slow one's progress and the lessons meant to be learned here will have to wait until a later time. At the core of our being, we wish to create and create and create, always learning, always discovering, always expanding our awareness. If past life research is not helping in this regard then why bother with it? But if it is helping to develop these things, then by all means, utilize this knowledge to the greatest extent you are able.

Just words

For the person you see in the mirror
there are many more awaiting your approval.

For the good deeds you apply
There are a million more thoughts you're not sure of.

Expression picks and chooses its release
based on approval of the front.

Only a front;
Only the current version of yourself,
That is all.

Just a chosen first-runner for today.

Take no offense that these wise words belong
to anyone who will hear them
They are not yours.

And the ones you spoke earlier -
The ones you disapproved of

They are not yours either.

— Michelle Senjem

Michelle Senjem and Rebecca LeTourneau

Readings: A Psychic at Work

As far back as I can remember I have had this tendency to take on a nurturing mother role with those around me. Even the neighbor kids who didn't know me all that well would seek out my advice on various issues, such as how to convince their parents to let them do something, or if they should join this or that club, or why so and so was mad at them, and so forth. My friends, certainly, came to me with their problems, hoping I would be able to see something they were missing. It seemed so natural at the time I didn't really think much about it but as I grew into adulthood and had my own children, I began to think more and more about the psychic aspects of my nature until finally deciding it was something I should give more energy to.

Still, I couldn't have been more surprised when people actually began to offer me money to share my impressions with them. Such a thing had never occurred to me! But as I proceeded to comply with these requests, daring to think of it as my livelihood, more and more people heard about me and sought out my services.

Eventually, a wonderful woman named Dee offered to rent me a small room in her new age shop so I could perform readings for people full time. I was overwhelmed by this idea at first but figured it must be the right path for me since it came about so easily and felt so right. I was also very impressed with Dee, who rented all her rooms for a very reasonable price, her greatest intention being simply to help and support local psychics. So, I joined the other, more experienced 'readers' who had been in business for a long time and hoped it would turn out okay.

At first I was anxious, feeling very pressured to perform well for these people I did not know. What if they did not like me? What if they resented what I had to say? I even doubted my own abilities, wondering if I would be able to read them correctly, even though I knew I had help from the spirit realm; what if my own ego got in the way too much and messed everything up?

But I spent some time in meditation conversing with my guides and soon I was doing readings for people in a professional setting just as I used to do for friends and acquaintances in my living room. It really was no different at first. I enjoyed helping people out with their concerns and was interested in the many different spirits who revealed themselves to me while performing readings. Most of the people who came into my little room there in Dee's shop had their own guides around them who were eager to help. Many times, the clients were blocked from recognizing these guides themselves but usually their guides would assist me anyway, telling me what to say so that the client would understand what needed to be addressed.

Many times when this happened, I would not understand the visions or symbols I was seeing at all. They would make no sense to me whatsoever but they always had some significance for the client. Other times, the messages I got would be so silly and filled with ridiculous images I had a hard time keeping myself from collapsing into hysterical giggles right there on the spot. It began to dawn on me that spirits often use humor to convey messages to humans; they love to hear us laugh!

One very thin and worn-out woman named Opal came to see me one time who had been through a serious illness and was having trouble readjusting to working life after being laid up for so long. She complained about her co-workers, saying they had a lack of compassion for her condition and wondered if she should quit and try to find something else to do.

"I can hardly get out of bed in the morning," she said, in a high, whining voice, "even though the doctor says I am healthy now. I think he might be missing something."

I sat across from her, quietly meditating on her surrounding energy. All at once a pair of ghostly dancing figures appeared just above her head. They looked like little, round weebils with short stubby legs and their faces were contorted in laughter. They held their fat little stomachs and bent forward, seemingly unable to speak. I didn't say anything for a moment. This woman was obviously distressed; how could I tell her there were these little beings above her, laughing their heads off?

Careful to keep a straight face, I sent the little figures a question through my mind. I wanted to know what to say to this poor woman!

"Say Italy," one of them said, clutching his sides, "say ITALY!"

"Uh ... Italy," I said.

"What did you say?" Opal asked, frowning.

"Well, I see these ... these forms above your head and they are telling me to say 'Italy' to you."

She didn't say anything, just kind of stared at me. Great, I thought, these guys are going to get me in trouble.

"Tell her the plane isn't the monster - Bessie is!" the other tiny figure screamed at me. God, I thought, these spirits are crazy.

"Tell her, tell her," they both yelled, still laughing and bobbing around. I thought they looked like beach balls in an invisible ocean, the way they were rising and falling so easily in the air.

"They say the plane isn't the monster," I said, "but Bessie is."

I held my breath, waiting for Opal to storm out of there in disgust. But she didn't. Instead, she clasped both hands to her cheeks and stared at me with round eyes. I asked her if these things meant anything to her.

"Of course," she said, her voice filled with wonder. "Bessie is the nickname we gave our copy machine at work. You know, I hate that copy room. I hate that whole place."

"Why do you work somewhere that makes you feel that way?" I asked her, gently.

She sighed. "I don't know. I've been there so long. My boss has been real understanding about my being sick - took me back after all that time off..."

"Italy," shrieked the little beings above her head, "Italy, Italy, Italy!"

"They keep saying something about Italy," I told her, not mentioning the fact that they appeared to be screaming at the top of their lungs.

"That's so weird," she said. "I had kind of given up on that idea."

"What idea?"

"Well," she explained, "I used to be really involved with this man ... it was a couple of years ago. We were even talking about getting married and everything. But then he got this offer from his uncle to go and work at a computer company in Italy where his parents and his brother live, and he just ... went."

"He just took off and left you?"

"Well, he did ask me to go with him but I thought, I can't just pick up and move to Italy. I don't speak Italian or anything, how could I do that? So I told him to forget it and then, not long after he left I got so sick I kind of put the whole thing out of my mind."

"Do you have any way to get in touch with him?" I asked her, feeling that we were on to something.

"See, that's the thing," Opal said, her voice cracking a bit. "I just got a postcard from him about a month ago. He said, 'still waiting for you to change your mind.' God, that's so weird."

"But you still don't want to go?"

"I don't know. It's such a big transition. All the way across the ocean..."

"She's afraid of the plane," one of the little guys told me, "because of her parents. She keeps that fear all wrapped up inside her skin."

"Did your parents die in a plane crash?" I asked her.

124

"Oh, my god," she said. She sat back in her seat, covering her face with her hands. After a bit she told me that yes, her parents had died in a plane crash and she had always been extremely afraid of flying. It came out that she was resisting the idea of going to Italy more because of the plane trip than because of the major change in language and culture. I assured her that her guides would not let anything happen to her on this trip. If she took a plane to Italy, she would get there safe and sound. I also told her that her illness had a lot to do with this fear she had because she had allowed it to keep her from pursuing the one relationship that felt perfect to her. She had given up the only true love she had ever known because she was afraid to fly. It also became clear to Opal that she had begun to despise her job more and more ever since receiving that postcard the month before. She knew at some level that she wanted to go and was angry with herself for not being able to take the plunge.

Fascinated, I encouraged her to follow her heart and as we talked, I watched her transform right before my eyes into a bright-eyed, smiling woman, the picture of health. Her skin seemed to glow and the tired circles under her eyes began to fade dramatically.

"I can already see the change in you," I told her. "You need to go where you feel drawn to and have faith that you will be taken care of. You're not alone, you know."

"I know," she said, tears in her eyes. "I can already feel how right it is. I'm going to go right home and call him."

"I think he's waiting," I said.

"He would be," she said, and laughed. I commented on how nice it was to see her laughing and happy.

"Yeah," she replied, with a wistful smile. "You know, nobody ever made me laugh like Stephen did."

That was a very gratifying experience for me and I was overjoyed a few weeks later when a postcard from Opal came to the shop. She said she was having the time of her life there in Italy; she loved the countryside and had never felt better in her life. What a high I was on! It felt so great to be able to help people, to assist them in seeing what they already knew but had just blocked out for some reason. I often think of those strange little creatures above Opal's head, too, laughing at the way they had given me the help I needed in such a funny and unorthodox way.

Every reading, of course, did not go so well. Sometimes, the sessions were very stressful. People came to me with severe problems, some of them, and I would get very stressed, unable to stop their sorrow and pain from affecting me physically. I would get headaches and at times would get sick with a sore throat or with some strange flu that lasted for days. Still, I felt strongly that I was doing some very important work so I struggled through these times, continuing to seek the assistance I needed from my own spirit guides.

After I had been doing these readings at Dee's shop for some time, I began to acquire quite a following and was asked to write an ongoing advice column in a local new age paper called *The Edge*. This gave me the freedom to share my insights with others without feeling the stress of their problems directly. I enjoyed doing this work but the person-to-person readings still took up the bulk of my time and energy.

In performing readings for people, I began to see beings of light floating about the room during some of my sessions. I could feel that these beings were extremely intelligent and was greatly humbled by this because I understood immediately that they were far more advanced than I in knowledge and insight. They would hover about, impressing upon my mind the subjects most important to the client at that time even though the client would sometimes be talking about something completely different.

The light beings in the room would fade a little bit at times if they felt it was too soon to approach a given subject and other times they would motion to me with hand gestures to convey certain ideas. It was like a sign language of sorts, but a very unique one, since I understood what they were communicating right away even though I had never received messages from such hand signals before.

It helped a great deal to have these beings of light present during readings since I was often feeling stressed out by the serious nature of many subjects my clients would bring up. This spiritual presence in the room served to calm me and gave me a great sense of comfort in that I knew they would be able to direct me through the session no matter how sticky it became. They were always patient and kind, sometimes funny, sometimes very serious, but always loving and interested and helpful. With some clients they would just kind of hover unobtrusively in the background as they had with Opal and other beings or spirits would reveal themselves. Other times, these beings of light would be the only spiritual presence I could sense in the room and would play a central role in the entire reading.

These loving light beings taught me so much about patience and compassion I became much better at reading others, even those people in my own life I often had trouble with because of the way I viewed them in general. I would get impatient at times when I saw people repeating destructive patterns over and over again or when they would refuse to acknowledge their own role in the problems in their lives. Through the perspective of these light beings I was continually reminded of what Baji had told me about these people having much to teach us. They helped me to keep in mind that all people are creating some very valuable things at many different levels, even when their lives seem chaotic and wasteful. I learned to feel love and acceptance of those people, both in my personal life and at work, who were severely blocked from their own emotions and who were determined to remain in a victim role. The graceful nature of these light beings was highly inspirational to me as I saw how patiently they awaited the unfolding of truth and freedom within conflicted human souls.

One of the times these light beings helped me a great deal happened during a reading I was doing for a woman in her sixties named Martha. She had been plagued throughout her life by a fear she just couldn't identify. Her many medical problems through the years had been associated with her female organs and she felt she had always had problems with sexuality. However, as open as she was about these issues, she seemed unable or unwilling to investigate any emotional cause for such troubles.

As the light beings in the room instructed, I moved forward to place my hands gently on her shoulders and when I did, I suddenly saw the image of a man fondling the genitals of a female toddler as he removed her diaper! I was shocked. I felt very strongly that I could not tell her what I had seen. I was not a licensed therapist - how could I open so deep a wound if this woman didn't even remember its existence!

In my despair, I suddenly felt the comforting presence of the light beings whispering into my ears. They informed me that I was correct in holding back from telling Martha what I had seen. Instead, I was to lead her gently back into childhood memories of a more general nature. This exercise was difficult enough for her and she did not remember too much that day but she did mention feeling very fearful of her father.

After a bit of this, the light beings again directing me, I gently led her to focus on specific areas of her body. I encouraged her to listen to the cells in these areas, informing her that they each had a story to tell. Through this exercise, Martha suddenly announced that she had *never* been comfortable with her father. At that moment, the light beings began to fade and I knew I was not to pursue this subject any further so I ended the session. It had been an hour and a half since we had begun so it was a relief for me to bring it to a close. Martha and I engaged in a short meditation to set our thoughts at ease for the time being and when we finished she seemed much more relaxed and at peace with herself.

Two weeks later, Martha returned to inform me that she had been having recurring visions of being molested as a child by somebody.

"It was a man," she said, thoughtfully. "I think it might have been my father."

I encouraged her to seek counseling, which she promised she would, but already I could see the difference in her demeanor. She said she felt that a vague and insistent fear had left her.

"I feel tired, more than anything," she said, laughing a bit, "as if I just ran a marathon or something."

I was amazed by Martha's experience, especially by the way she had received the healing she needed through focusing her energy on her body. I thanked the light beings for this; once again they had taught me a new way to approach problems, a new way to find the answers to upsetting questions. It occurred to me that I should be engaging in this sort of activity myself, since I seemed to be feeling sick so often. However, what we can sometimes see so clearly in others, we often miss in ourselves and even though my intentions were sincere, I was not yet ready to face the truth about what was making me ill.

Meanwhile, as I was trying to figure this out, another very moving experience happened during a reading I did with Esther, a woman who came to me in a state of distress, saying she desperately needed the help of some healing angels. At fifty-some years old, she appeared much older, her face filled with the lines of worry and sleepless nights and an endless torrent of anguished tears.

Apparently, Esther's son had been killed in a motorcycle accident about two years prior and she was having a most difficult time letting go of him. I listened in sympathy as she described how he had been so courageous and full of life, always involved with this or that activity, often playing the reckless daredevil.

"All those crazy things he did," she said, "and he never once got hurt."

Yet, one night when she was feeling ill she asked him to go to the drugstore and pick up some medicine for her. As always, he was happy to help. He hopped on his motorcycle and roared off in the usual way, only this time his ride was ended in a mass of tangled metal on the side of the road.

As Esther spoke, I began to see the wavering outline of her son standing just beyond her alongside the wall. He began communicating with me immediately and I relayed this information to Esther as he said it, sure that it would comfort her greatly.

"He's telling you that he was fearful of this world," I said, "and that he lived so dangerously because of this - he wanted to leave this physical existence because he saw only frightening things here. He says it is not your fault, not in the least. He was just not ready for this earthly experience and wanted to go back into the safety of the spirit world."

"That's not him you're seeing," Esther snapped, shaking her head. "He would never say such things! My boy was never afraid of anything in his life. Even as a very young child he would climb right to the top of tall trees without a moment's hesitation. Something's wrong with your vision, Michelle. I killed him, that's all. I killed him and I know it. That's why he's gone!"

I sighed and listened again to what her son was saying. He had taken the form of a lightly glowing being near the wall, tall and slender and calm.

"He says that he is fine," I went on, "and that he loves you and ... again, he is insisting that it is not your fault —"

"It *is* my fault!" Esther cried. "If I hadn't sent him out that night, he would still be with me!"

Helpless, I grew silent, not knowing how to help her. Obviously, she was not going to accept what her son was telling her. What should I do? I asked this question, desperately, to the light beings hovering in the back of the room. Immediately, they came forward and began to instruct me, gently.

"Sometimes," they told me, "a person's belief must simply be honored."

Confused but relieved that they were helping me, I began to speak in the manner they suggested. I told Esther that yes, it was her doing that her son was gone in that she had played a part in the manner in which he exited this world. As soon as the words were out of my mouth, Esther fell into a sobbing heap in my arms. She cried and cried, deep heart wrenching sobs for nearly three hours as I held her. Finally, she regained her composure and breathed a deep, shaky sigh.

"I can feel his forgiveness," she said, wiping her eyes.

"Yes," I told her, gently, "and now you must honor that by forgiving yourself."

She nodded, thanking me and left in a rather peaceful state, considering the way she had been when she arrived. I sank back into my chair, exhausted and stunned by this experience. Thankful that the light beings were still near, I questioned them. Why was this approach necessary? I would never have thought to honor Esther's need to punish herself when no punishment was necessary. But, the light beings informed me, sometimes this is the only path that will work effectively. Confused, I declared that my work had always been centered on a search for truth! Clearly, what had happened here today did not seem to be in alignment with the truth.

"Yes, but you see Michelle," the light beings told me, patiently, "this was *her* truth!"

Amazed, I thought about this and realized that each one of us is experiencing this earthly adventure in our own, unique way. What one of us sees and believes is not going to be the same as what another sees and believes. Yet we all feel we know what is true and what is not. How incredible it all is! Each of us so unique, so intricate in our design and yet we are all connected at a very deep level - how different are our paths toward the same truth! It may take many lifetimes and multi-dimensional experiences before Esther and I see things in the same light but we are all on the road to increasing enlightenment no matter what avenue we are taking. Our goal is one and the same - to become more and more of who we are, of who we *all* are in our creative potential - forever and ever through eternity.

Doing readings for others in this professional setting was a very insightful and moving experience for me in many ways. I came into contact with so many different kinds of people, some of whom were on very different paths than I was and held very different beliefs than I did. Still, I learned something from every session, whether or not it went well. Most people who came to see me were genuinely seeking information or help about some important issue in their lives but every once in a while a skeptic would walk through the door determined to reveal me as a fraud. I could always sense this immediately and would heave a sigh of impatience, thinking how much time was about to be wasted. However, I learned from these experiences as well. For one thing, if a person was not sincere in his or her questioning of me I would see no light beings, would feel no spiritual presence in the room - I just wouldn't get a thing.

"Sorry," I would say, "I'm not getting anything on that."

This seemed to surprise people but I have never had a problem being honest in this regard. If I am not picking up any information, I will just say so. If the person is honestly searching for answers and nothing comes to me, I assume it is just not time for them to know yet or they are supposed to receive their answers in a different way. There is no shame in this at all.

Some people seem to think that 'psychics' are always 'on' and will be able to see concrete answers to everything but this is not so. I know for sure it is not so with me and I highly doubt it is so with anyone. We are human after all. Just as you may feel more in tune and in flow some days than others, I can more easily pick up information at some times than others. A lot of it has to do with how centered I am, how much is going on in my own life at the time, how close I am feeling to my own spirit

132

guides or sometimes it depends on the person I am facing and what is going on in their own particular life adventure. I do know that I usually don't have to try too hard; if I am going to pick up some useful information for someone, I will sense it right away. I will just look around, waiting, keeping my mind and heart open, and will begin to see images or moving pictures almost immediately. Sometimes, they appear on walls or ceilings or carpet, sometimes in water or the sky or just in the air, and sometimes I will hear things or just see faces or places inside my head. If I am not going to sense anything I can usually tell this right away, also. The atmosphere just seems empty of anything but the physical and I do not feel that familiar shift happening which serves to open other dimensions to my vision.

I have many wonderful psychics in my day, but every once in a while, I will run into someone who experiences this lack of information coming through but will just make something up, afraid to admit there is nothing to see. When I was a young mother, one woman told me my husband was going to die within seven years and I was going to have another child, which I was going to have to raise on my own! This is a terrible thing to do to someone. For one thing, even if I did see something awful like this, I would not tell that person in such a blunt fashion. I may approach the subject in a roundabout way, urging them to focus on health issues or asking them to work at becoming more in touch with their own Spirit Circle. Also, predicting a death like this is never a sure thing because the future can always be changed. We can see probabilities or an emerging likelihood but we can never say for sure how something is going to go. This is because the act of living in the human realm is a project in motion, always shifting and changing along with one's thoughts and intentions - we always have the ability to change our course midstream and take off in a new direction. When we are in touch with our spiritual roots, these changes often occur abruptly or by strange coincidence because we are allowing our spiritual guides to help us along. How strongly one is connected to spirit will always have an impact on how the future plays out.

As I have said, we are all psychic to a certain extent and can all be more so if we focus our attention on developing this ability. You can try different things to improve in this area. While thinking of someone close to you, or even not so close to you, look for clues in your surrounding environment. Pay attention to the thoughts that drift through your mind while thinking of that person. The more you learn to trust your own intuition and the more you become alert to subtle messages appearing in the world around you, the easier it will become to tune into the energy of another and get information about them. Often, the messages will be quite general, as in a feeling that they are going through a rough period or are approaching some exciting turn of events but other times you may get something very specific, such as seeing a vision of a car accident or an image of this person meeting a new lover. Trust what you get and see what happens. With some practice and commitment, you will see that your 'hunches' get more and more accurate. Also, the more you determine to communicate with your own spirit guides and listen for their direction, the more you will hear, see, and sense their help in the reading of others.

One thing I would like to make clear because of concern expressed by many who visited me during those years of doing readings, is that I was never given any information they truly did not want me to know. Those things that they held private and secrets they did not wish to reveal stayed hidden within the cloak of their personal shields. Spirit honors such desires of privacy and will not usually yank aside a person's opposition to reveal what they do not wish at some level to reveal. I never heard, saw or sensed anything that would make a person feel humiliated or violated. Perhaps this is because I had no wish to do such a thing but I also think it was because the spirit guides around those people were careful to protect their physical soul-self from such an intrusion.

Any honorable work will include the respect of another's boundaries, even if those boundaries seem to exist in contrast to the beliefs of the 'psychic'. One thing I learned very clearly through Esther and others is that the belief systems of others should be respected and approached with care. I think, in my human way, that those who hold belief systems that hurt others are despicable. Yet I am also aware that spirit has use for many things I don't understand right now and I will not be able to see the whole picture from where I stand. So I simply choose not to go there. I stay in the realm of my own intentions and allow others to do the same. If I can help people, that's great. If I run up against someone who appears to be intent upon hurting others, I get away from them, choosing not to participate in their drama. Of course, if I can do something to stop them, I will. But I am not going to pretend I have the power to change the world around with my own desires and stop people from doing destructive things to others. I wish it didn't happen, but it does. And, if I am going to be here participating in this earthly adventure, I have to accept that. However, this doesn't mean I have to get caught up in whatever craziness they are creating because I have different plans for my time here this time around.

One thing I have noticed is that when you focus your energy on joy and learning and helping and healing, this is what will emerge more and more in your life. The people you come into contact with will be those you *will* be able to help, or perhaps they will help you. The more you create a positive energy field around yourself, the more you will attract this same energy from others. There may be some rough spots here and there, you may come up against some who are just not going to bring you anything but grief, but gradually these people will fade from your life more and more leaving you more room to focus on those who share in your bliss and your creative energy. Turn your attention to those people who uplift you or who genuinely benefit from your help. When you are truly helping someone you will feel it and you will see the change in him or her. They won't be continually repeating the same mistakes over and over; they will be changing and growing just as you are. With diligence and an ever-growing trust in spirit, you will find yourself participating more and more in a great wheel of joy and fun and exciting discovery. You will bump into more and more people who are participating in this same wheel and who appreciate your presence. You will be inspired by their insights and actions as they will be from yours and it will get easier and easier to let go of any excess baggage in the form of negative influences. Just let it go! You have better things to do, a more spiritual life to create, and many, many wonderful people out there waiting to become a part of your more balanced and joyful life.

For a long time, I continued to do readings at that little shop in Stillwater even though my physical condition seemed to be getting more and more susceptible to the ailments of others. This bothered me very much at a spiritual level because I felt that if I were living my life in alignment with my higher purpose and was in constant contact with those of my spirit circle, I shouldn't be suffering like I was. Everything else seemed to be going well; I was making a good living and was coming into contact with many different types of people, which is something I enjoy - so what was the problem? It seemed I was missing something. Obviously my body was trying to get my attention. I thought perhaps it was just that I needed to develop my reading skills enough so that I could remain more detached and not take on the physical and emotional pain of others, but no matter how hard I tried to do this I couldn't seem to rectify the situation.

One day, after many attempts to glean messages about this problem from those of my Spirit Circle, Baji visited me again. I could feel him in the room, this time in the form of a hazy, purple mass of energy that hovered above my kitchen table, then moved slowly toward me until it surrounded me. As always, I felt a warmth and peace flooding through me. Without speaking, I put down the bowl I had been wiping clean and went into the front room to sit on the sofa. Immediately, I was relaxed. No deep breathing necessary this time!

I could feel Baji's energy hovering there, around me and through me, and I felt light and heavy at the same time. Rooted to the spot, yet I could hardly feel my body.

"You're dodging your feelings," he said. His voice sounded like water, or like something under water. It was kind of like a soft whispering inside my head, yet around me at the same time.

"What do you mean?" I asked.

"You want to kid around and make jokes instead of looking at what is going on inside you. It is okay to look, Michelle. Don't be afraid. Take a moment."

I quieted my thoughts, turning my attention inward. What did I feel like? I thought over the past few hours, days, weeks. All the frustration of not knowing exactly what to do. In one sense, I felt compelled to do readings for people; I knew I was able to help many of them. Yet doing readings was making me sick. I kept on getting headaches, backaches, and some mornings I could hardly drag myself out of bed to go back there and do readings again. Something was wrong.

"I feel like I don't want to do readings anymore," I said, "at least not professionally. The money is good but it is making me feel sick. I don't feel like I used to about it; I feel like it's a struggle now just to get myself motivated to *want* to read people!"

"And yet..." Baji said, encouraging me to continue.

"Well," I paused, thinking, "...I guess I just... well, I feel conflicted because my beliefs are so strong and I so want to share what I experience with others. I look out there and see so many people who would be much, much happier, whose lives would be so much easier, if they could only see the magnitude of their own spirits. If they could only accept themselves for who they are right now. Doing readings for people is one way I can introduce people to their guides, to the spirits around them. It is a way I can help them to understand that there is a spiritual dimension around them that is affected by everything they do and everything they think. I feel like it is really important work."

"But it is making you sick. So, apparently a part of you is letting you know that this is not where you truly want to be. Deep in your spirit, you have other plans."

"But what other plans? And why would I be getting sick by something I believe is so vital?"

"You said doing readings for people is *one* way you can share what you have learned with others. So listen to yourself, Michelle. If this is only one way, then surely there are other ways you can share what you know and see."

"How?" I asked, thoroughly confused.

"You want me to give you definite and concrete answers right away, don't you," Baji said, kindly. "This is not uncommon, I'm afraid. So many of you in the human form insist upon getting absolute answers to your questions right away. Otherwise, you doubt the validity of Spirit; you become angry or depressed and make all sorts of destructive judgments about the world. It seems to be so very hard for many, if not most, humans to understand that you do not need to understand everything all at once. You really don't even want to, although you may think you do! The whole point of going into the human experience in the first place is to learn from the state of being in the unknown, in the uncertain adventure! If you already had full knowledge of everything, and you *could*, the human state would not have the impact it does. Being so intently focused on the physical plane lends itself to many a drama with great impact and emphasis on the emotional level."

"But why would we even come here to experience this physical life if we could already know everything beforehand?" I asked, confused.

"That is a very human question. I will try and explain, Michelle. You see, knowledge and growth is ever expanding, ever-growing. It is an eternal process. Becoming human and going through that experience is a part of the learning process; it is a very effective way to gain a perspective and insight that is only possible from outside the spiritual realm. Not that you aren't still connected, because you are. But you are approaching things from a temporary state, which is very different from the way things are seen from where I am, *and* from where you are when you are in spirit."

"Okay," I said, smiling a little, "so, now that I am here, tell me how I can get to where I want to go. Tell me how my life can be more joyful and easier. Tell me everything I need to know."

The quiet chuckle in my ear and in my head made me feel warm all over. True happiness swept over me as I basked in the knowledge that I had made Baji laugh.

"Yes, this is another very common request from the human experience," he said. "But again, to know everything at once is not how you wished it. If life were always easy you would have no reason to seek out the spiritual connection that helps you accomplish what you came here to accomplish. You wouldn't feel motivated to learn much of anything new."

"Oh, all right. I get it," I said, with an exaggerated sigh. "So, tell me, if you can, what did I come here to learn?"

"You came here to accomplish what every human being came here to accomplish, Michelle. You came here to learn how to further your creative powers."

"To further my creative powers..."

"Yes. You see, being a part of God or the Great Creator or whatever you want to call the ALL, involves the act of creating. What else would a Creator do? You see we all yearn to create for this is the force of life. Creativity is the simplest fact of life, of nature; it is the force that makes everything else happen.

You feel unhappy with your current situation, Michelle, because it is not where your creative expression lies at this time. It is not in the interest of your true nature right now. You see, the more you are aligned with your true nature, the more firmly you are rooted in the most powerful point of creativity. The way to recognize your true nature is to pay close attention to what holds your interest. So, ask yourself, what are you interested in these days?"

"Well..." I thought for a moment, "...I'm interested in spirits, in past lives, in metaphysical phenomena..."

"Yes, yes, but I want you to take a moment and really think back to the past few weeks, Michelle. What seems to be holding your attention much of the time lately?"

I squinted, thinking. Hmm. Sure, I was still reading inspiring material wherever I could find it; I still sought out the help and advice of my guides and played with tarot cards but it was true that I had also been heavily involved with my children as of late. I was spending more and more time at their school volunteering and had made many friends there, both among students and the faculty.

"Aha," Baji said, "now, do you see where your energy has been directed?"

"Yeah," I said, surprised. "I really like spending time at the school. It makes me feel closer to my kids. And you know, there are so many kids there who need attention. I can't believe how many of them seem so lost and disconnected from their own parents and families. These are great kids too, most of them. But they get treated like juvenile delinquents - like they are teenagers already. Though I don't understand why so many parents think their teenagers are such a problem, either. I think it's going to be fun when Chris and Jill are teenagers."

"Do you have some sort of belief that contributing to this world of school and needy children is somehow less valuable than the work you do in giving readings to people?" Baji asked.

"Uh... no! I mean, maybe..." I stopped, frowning again. Maybe I *had* been thinking this at some level. Maybe I was caught up in the notion that psychic work was more spiritually important that the practical, everyday work of dealing with kids in the school system.

"Yet," Baji said, "dealing and working with young people in the way that you do is very important indeed. You are affecting lives just as much, albeit by a different method. In actuality, you are having the same effect - you are assisting people in their own awakening to their own paths of creativity. This is the purpose, ultimately, of any kind of help whatsoever."

"Ah... I guess I might have been thinking... I don't know, like I had this gift..."

"And you should be using it, I know. But do you see how funny that is? Developing the insight to see into other people's thoughts and feelings or as humans say, being psychic, is no different from the insight and kindness needed to relate to troubled children. Meaning, it is no more or less special.

Everyone is psychic, just as everyone has kindness in them and the ability to relate to young people but not everyone will be tuned in to this part of themselves. The key is to go where your interests pull you. If your intent is pure and you are a seeker, your interests will always pull you to a place that is more closely aligned with your true nature, thus will always lead you to a situation where you are better able to express your creativity."

"So... I should just quit doing readings and volunteer all the time at the school?" I asked, incredulously. "How will we pay the bills?

Again, that soft chuckle washed over me.

"Ah, the money thing. Yes, you could choose to see this as a problem. But, you see, if you are following your interests honestly the universe will assist you in giving you the support that you need. You must trust this process. Let those interests of yours flow through you and validate their importance by thinking positively about them. Your own ability to create situations in your life is unlimited, you see. The greatest hindrance you will encounter is simply fear. Watch your thoughts, Michelle, just for one day, and see how much time you actually spend on inspiring ideas and notions as opposed to how much time you spend on other, more negative thoughts. You may be a bit taken aback at what you find!"

"I worry too much," I said, nodding.

"Most people, even the most optimistic people, spend more than enough time in worry to create a challenge or two so don't be surprised that you have not created everything you want in your life yet. Every thought and feeling that you have attaches to something of life's vibration, you see. That is not to say that every fearful or worrisome thought is dangerous but if you have a vast number of these you will create a vibrational range that can make it difficult for positive situations to manifest themselves around you."

"So, I have to control my thoughts more," I said with a sigh.

"I am not talking about control so much as choice. You always have a choice, whether to think this way or that. It should help you to know that you carry with you, at all times, the tremendous force of creative potential. Always, the beliefs, desires, patterns and possibilities are within you that can lead you to where you want to be. Many times, problems come from the habit of making things too complicated, from trying to analyze things too much with the logical parts of the brain instead of just calming down and listening to your body. Where do you want to be? What brings you joy? What holds your interest? You are capable of much, much more than worry but you must set yourself free to express the inherent knowing that lies within you. It is very, very simple. Look at the leaves blowing in the wind, to get an idea of what I am telling you. Watch the blooming flower. What is your natural state of being?"

I listened to this with some awe, feeling suddenly more content than I had in weeks. It didn't even matter any more that I didn't know what in the world I was going to do for income. I just knew I was about to take another path and that I was free to follow my yearnings, for they were the clues to who I really was and to my purpose in coming to this earth in human form. As soon as Baji spoke the words, I recognized their truth. Somewhere in the deep recesses of my being it made perfect sense.

"Everyone exists with endless possibilities," Baji said. "There are no time constraints in the universe in which to complete one's thinking and creative purpose. People, and sometimes spirits, get caught up in thinking along linear lines, attaching some sort of time line not only to themselves but also to those around them. This is not necessary. Think of this moment right now as eternity. For, you see, eternity is at the core of each and every moment. It underlies every single experience, always and forever within you. Relax. Stop and allow love to flow through you right here, right now. Let it carry you along on the waves of this illusion we call Time, for then you will exist closer to the center of your being."

The purple energy was gone then, leaving me as suddenly as it had come. Still, I sat on the sofa for a long time afterward, soaking up what I had just heard and experienced. How blessed I was to have such direction!

Yet, I knew even as I thought this that all of us here on earth have this direction around us every moment of every day. We simply have to tune in to our own true natures and pay attention to that which calls to us. In this, our beauty and power of creativity is revealed. Even though I was to forget this many times later on, getting caught up in this worry or that, it was very, very clear to me at that moment.

I had no idea what I was going to do about work but as I sat there basking in this incredible experience I had just been through, it didn't even matter. I believed with all of my being that what I had just been told was true and I trusted that things would work themselves out somehow. All I had to do was be true to my own authentic being! How simple it sounded, how too-good-to-be-true it seemed. Yet, as I was soon to find out, Baji was right. The universe and the flow of life did support me in my transition from doing the readings to another avenue of expression, even though it was not at all in the way I expected!

Wind rushes by
Swiftly and soundless
It relishes the launch into Eternity
(where we will go)
The wind will bring us to our home

Michelle Senjem and Rebecca LeTourneau

The Creator Within

With Baji's gentle guidance I stopped doing readings even though I had no idea how I was going to earn money. I threw my energy into volunteering full time at the elementary school Chris and Jill attended. I knew I would have to bring in an income eventually so I simply visualized myself working in an office environment with lots of books and papers around and with little people (children) nearby. I didn't get any more specific than this, for I was not sure of anything further. What I was sure about, I visualized and expected. The How and When of it all, I left up to my higher selves to figure out.

One day as I was helping a group of children form the appointed lines in the hallway, one of the school officials approached me saying there was a position opening up at the school that would be perfect for me. The school needed someone to head up a parent volunteer center and since I was already so involved in the system it should be right up my alley. I wasn't sure I would get the job but went and applied anyway, figuring it must have flown in front of my face for a reason! Also, it sounded wonderful to be able to continue working at the kids' school while getting paid for it! I tried not to let doubts or insecurities seep in and tried not to imagine what other kinds of people I would be competing against. Instead, I concentrated on turning my worries over to Spirit, expecting that they would help me create exactly what I wanted.

As it turned out, I was the only one who applied for the job! Ecstatic, I threw myself into the work with gusto and gratitude, changing it to fit my own vision. I set up programs that involved troubled teens coming in from the high school to help out the younger kids and get credit for doing so, knowing that many of them only needed some help in realizing their own potential. Most of these troubled teens had never been trusted with responsibility before in such a meaningful way and rose to the occasion beautifully. I loved working with teenagers; we seemed to have a natural rapport. Other schools got wind of this program and contacted us to learn how to implement it in their own districts. Once again, I felt as though I were in alignment with my intended path. Just as doing readings had taught me so much about life and about myself, so did working with kids and parents in the schools. Life is not static. We are always moving and changing and to become stuck where we are no longer interested will only serve to deaden our soul connection. I was very glad I had moved when I felt it prudent, even though I needed a push from Baji to do it!

One interesting thing I noticed when changing my environment was the very different nature of the people I was surrounded by each day. While working at the new age shop, I had been around people who were very interested in things of a metaphysical nature and this had usually been the focus of our conversations and thoughts. At the school, I was around people who had very different interests, many of them never giving a thought to metaphysical phenomena. Consequently, my interactions with them took on a different tone and I was led to learn many lessons that would not have arisen in my previous work environment. Still, as I soon found out, the people who did have an interest in things of a spiritual nature began to drift toward me from all angles. Before long, I was even giving readings to people at the school! It seemed I was not going to be separated from this aspect of my nature no matter where I went.

So, even while working in a much different place and doing things not at all associated with psychic talents, I was led to do the same type of reading work I had been doing before. The wonderful difference was that I was not limited to this. I could learn about and discover many other lessons and dimensions of life. I was also not bound by anything; I was free to pick and choose who I would do readings for and when I would do them. There was no obligation since I wasn't scheduled to take clients on any regular basis. Thus, I felt I had the best of both worlds! I could continue my spiritual development and my healing abilities while at the same time working in a very down-to-earth setting close to my children and helping those at-risk teens I found so irresistible.

Finding myself in such a joyous place made me believe I could create whatever I wanted in my life. All I had to do was focus my intentions, keep myself close to Spirit and then let it emerge miraculously around me. I felt I had found my center and could never be shaken from it again.

I was wrong.

It was a few years later that I woke up to the sound of a ringing phone. Blurry-eyed, I turned over to grasp at the receiver, noting with my dull senses that it was three in the morning. Who in the world would be calling at this hour? Glancing across the bed told me that Bruce had already left for work as was his pattern when things were getting sticky down at the store. I sighed at the possibility that his old van had broken down again. It was freezing outside. The previous night we had experienced one of the worst ice storms in recorded history and I was not in any hurry to get out there and participate in the January night myself.

However, it wasn't Bruce's voice I heard on the other end of the line. It was a lieutenant from the St. Paul police department. As soon as he announced his title, I feared the worst - that my son, who was nearly eighteen now, had collided with disaster in a fast-moving car. Why did those boys feel so compelled to show off all the time?

"I am arresting your son, ma'am," the lieutenant said," on a charge of attempted murder."

"*What?*"

"Yes, that's right," he said. A boy had been shot and now Chris had been found at a small party in a motel room where the suspect was hanging out also.

"We're still here at the motel, ma'am," the voice spoke kindly into my ear, "and your son is right here beside me. Would you like to say something to him?"

I couldn't believe my ears! But now there was Chris' shaking voice on the telephone line whispering assurances to me that of course he hadn't been involved in shooting anyone.

"Don't hurry to the police station, ma'am," the policeman said, taking the phone back from Chris. "It's very icy out and besides, it will take us another hour or so to get back there ourselves. So, you be careful, okay?"

His kindness touched me. Obviously, he could sense how distraught I was even though I had hardly said a thing. Also, I felt strongly that he sensed Chris' innocence because the way he treated my son suggested this. He was kind and patient and soothing, helping Chris through the questioning process and the transition to the police station, going out of his way to make sure Chris was comfortable. I think he realized after one look at Chris' face, that the young man was truly shocked about the whole thing.

Thankfully, Patty offered to drive me downtown that morning. I was so distraught, I didn't trust my own driving and the icy roads were not much of a comfort. As I rode next to Patty, my thoughts were all on Chris and the gentle nature of his soul. How would he ever deal with something like imprisonment? I knew he couldn't, it would be devastating for him, he would never be able to live through it... oh, I cried and cried in that car, unable to bear the thought of Chris behind bars.

"Oh, god," I moaned to Patty, "I had that dream... that dream..."

I had forgotten but now it was coming back to me, much to my horror. In the dream I had looked out my window to see a vehicle I didn't recognize parked in my driveway. As I went closer to investigate, a horrible scene unfolded before me: a young boy sat slumped over the wheel, thick red blood pouring from his head and chest. As I stared in horror, he turned and looked at me, saying, "you have to find Chris, he isn't safe either."

These words sent me screaming down the street in search of my son just as I was now hurtling toward the St. Paul Police station in the wee hours of morning, my heart in my throat.

When we finally arrived, Patty and I were directed toward an officer who, in a none too friendly fashion, proceeded to tell us the details of the crime. I was horrified to learn that the boy who had been shot was a childhood friend of Chris', someone he had gone to grade school with. Apparently, one of the bullets had entered the base of the neck exiting in the forehead area and another had gone through the chest - the boy was in surgery even as we spoke.

"But Chris would never hurt anyone," I told the police officer, desperately, "especially not a good friend of many years!"

"Well, I hope you're right," he replied, coolly.

"I'm telling you, it's not possible!" I insisted. Still, I combed through the phone book, calling everyone I knew, asking for information about the best lawyer we could find. I finally got a number to hold onto; the man said he was on call, waiting for me to summon him. Meanwhile, my son and husband had both arrived at the police station at the exact same time so I left the phone and hurried to speak with them. I have never seen Chris so distraught as he was that day. It was clear to me he was in shock because of the slow way he was moving; his brain was barely able to comprehend what was going on. He tried bravely to respond to a barrage of questions, many of which were hurled at him in accusatory tones.

Finally, the kind lieutenant who had spoken to me on the phone earlier approached Bruce and me where we were waiting in the hall.

"We're pretty certain your son has told us the truth," he said, patting my arm. "He seems like a very honest young man. Guess he was just in the wrong place at the wrong time."

He told us we could take him home with us! Bruce and I were ecstatic. Nearly four hours had passed since we arrived there at the station and all sorts of horrid worries had dominated my thinking during that time. Now, here was Chris walking toward us, still looking shocked and white, ready for us to take him home. As we walked toward the door, a policeman who had been with Chris in the back room stepped forward and threw his coat over our son's shoulders.

"Here," he said, "take this. It's pretty cold out there."

Comforted by this policeman's gesture and by the kindness of the lieutenant, we went home to try and sort out what happened. The nightmare was not over until the boy who was shot began to recover and revealed that Chris' story was true, that he hadn't been involved - the shooting had come about because of a disagreement between the victim and the suspect - both friends of Chris'.

When Chris had run into the suspect that night, he could sense the boy was desperate for company so he stayed with him wanting to show that he cared and remained with him long after his gut told him to go home. He had no idea what the kid had done but felt there was something wrong. Of course, when he realized what had happened, he was horrified and shocked, hardly able to believe one of his friends could do such a thing.

As for me, I was beside myself with terror throughout this entire experience. After it was finally over, I sought out Baji in a fit of anger. Why would I create such an experience? Why on earth would I be willing to participate in such a revolting drama? If I had a choice about everything I went through, why on earth would I choose something so awful as this?

"Think back," Baji said, calmly. "What kinds of thoughts have been running through your mind the past few weeks and months?"

It took some time before I was able to admit to myself that yes, I had worried about the time Chris spent in the city, wishing he would just stay out in our own neighborhood. I had also sensed things at times, which I did relay to my son but felt there was really nothing I could do to change Chris' behavior; he was almost an adult now and not willing to take orders from me. This lack of control created a helpless feeling within me, causing me to worry incessantly. And then there was that dream...

Baji: Scenarios are often created out of fear but even these events will hold useful lessons for all souls involved at some point. Not all things in your life are created by conscious thought. You also show your preferences toward specific events/results in your sleep. This gets trickier and demands a deep and unwavering trust in yourself - your Higher Self - and in all the networking you do with all of creation. Trust is the single most important facet to your happiness: trust in life, trust in guidance - the guidance of your children, your animals - trust in **all** *of life.*

Some of the problems Michelle had with her children served to uncover buried grief within her and forced her to face some of her greatest fears. Also, everyone who co-creates with you has their own reasons for what they do - you have simply agreed at some level of your being to participate in their earthly drama with them, as they have agreed to participate in yours. People are always creating their own realities as they go, by tuning into patterns and waves of energy - both mass and individual - and it matters greatly what one thinks and feels. Yes, you have sketched out a design for yourself before you came here but you are also free to alter the design, add to it or subtract; you are not bound by anything from the past or future.

This may be hard to fathom in some situations, especially when you feel so strongly that you want things to be **different** *than they are, but just because you can't imagine creating something in your life doesn't mean you didn't do it. Each of us exists in many levels of awareness at the same time. At each of these levels we are all creating and conducting various projects of creativity. We will be conscious of some of these, we may feel* *the hazy edges of others in hints and vague familiarities, but others we will have absolutely no notion of whatsoever within our conscious minds. How worthy a person feels, the waking visions and thoughts and views a person holds - these and other aspects alter the higher visions when they come into your consciousness, often changing their original intent and making them distorted. Therefore, you will get only pieces of your soul level intentions scattered into your beliefs and into your conscious versions of what you yearn for, what you want.*

There may be situations in which you are participating in someone's drama but realize that you no longer wish to be a part of this. If this is true, then you are perfectly free to disengage yourself. Likewise, others may detach themselves from whatever drama you are playing out. If you are persistent in your own interests, this will not alter your plans; you will simply find another participant down the road.

It matters what you think is possible. What you think you deserve has a profound impact on what you will get, also, both in material goods and in love relationships, as well as in everything in between. How much time and energy you give to a particular thought or idea will determine how easily it will come into fruition. This is true for the negative as well as for the positive - if you spend an excessive amount of time in worry, you are fueling the greater possibility of something happening in your life in response to this. Also, when you are worrying about someone you are not helping that person because you are sending out negative energy only. If you want to protect or assist people in their lives, send them strengthening thoughts and energy. Feed them positive messages about themselves: that they can handle things, that they are powerful beings, that they are supported on all sides, etc.

It will help you to realize that you can let go of your worries, sending them to your Higher Selves, allowing your conscious self to disengage from them, for Spirit has a much broader vision and is better equipped to deal with such things. Remember, you are the physical guide right now, being in the earthly realm. You are the point of interest for your Higher Selves right now. All of you would like nothing better than to please yourself!

Allowing, trusting, and feeding information via thoughts and feelings to your higher selves is the key to all forms of physical materialization from the human perspective. What you give out is what will come back to you, however differently created. It may not look or feel the same but when you delve deeply into situations you will find that yes, you did have a hand in setting up that scenario.

Your original intent and design, which you put together before entering the earth realm, comes to you in the form of inspirational, pulls in this direction or that. Even if you are not paying attention and are ignoring these pulls of your soul, life will throw situations at you to nudge you or sometimes knock you right over the head, trying to get your attention. This does not mean you have no choice in the matter and are doomed to buckle under to your pre-destined design no matter what, but it does mean you have sent yourself into this world with a clear direction of some sort in mind. You can change this direction by virtue of current intentions; you can refuse your own creative design in many ways. But if you try to go it alone like this, dismissing your higher vision, life came become very difficult. Every move you make will seem unclear and lonely, and you will often feel as though you are floundering in a sea of misunderstandings. In human form, you just don't have all the information you need to make every decision without the benefit of the vision from your higher selves.

As I began to accept my part in that terrifying scenario, I noticed more and more that I was too quick to attach fear to my children. This was obviously not helping them, so I worked to make my thoughts more empowering when thinking of them. I turned my worries over to those of my Spirit Circle, my higher selves, knowing they could handle them better than I.

Chris, who was very shook up from this experience, decided to go into the navy rather than piddle his life away in the city. How strange it was to have him suddenly decide this, then watch as he stuck to his guns and went off to boot camp. My son was leaving home! I was so happy on the one hand, for I had been very fearful of his ties to his old friends in the city, especially after that horrible shooting incident, but then on the other hand, I was lonely for Chris as soon as he stepped on that plane. What would I do without him?

It turned out that he absolutely loved boot camp. I had never heard anything like it before. I had always heard people grumbling about boot camp, making it through only by gritting their teeth and hanging on, but Chris reveled in it. I could hear it in his voice; he was happy! All of his life he had had the freedom to do what he wanted, to follow his own path pretty much, having his own feelings and intuition honored and now he was being ordered about, every little part of his life restricted by rigid rules and he loved it! I laughed and laughed at the irony of this, so proud of Chris I found it hard to stop talking about him. I bombarded everyone around me with stories about my son in boot camp who was having the time of his life.

I learn so much from my children, and in Chris I have seen a prime example of someone who creates his own world as he goes. He has become somewhat of a master at this, probably because he was allowed to do so from the time he came to us. Still, I am continuously amazed at the way he seems able to bend life to his will, implementing his desires so quickly in reality. That shooting incident really seemed to awaken this power in him, I think because he was so frightened by the consequences of *not* exercising his will over his own life. Once, while stationed south of Mexico, he told me about a person in his unit who constantly got on his nerves. This young man, for whatever reasons, was highly obnoxious, always trying to stir up trouble and to get people to react to his nonsense. Chris decided to handle this by simply ignoring his presence and by constantly visualizing this person gone from the ship. His intention was so focused that this young man was transferred off the ship within three days!

Another time, he noticed a job that looked desirable to him, that of LAN Administrator. He visualized himself in this job and focused his intent while continuing to give his all to the job he already had. Not long after, he was picked out of a crew of several hundred to fill this very position! It seemed the person holding the job had been shifted somewhere else - on the same ship even - leaving the job open for Chris, who had only been in the navy for nine months! Such a thing was relatively unheard of but for some reason Chris stood out in the minds of the officers and they plucked him out of the masses. I know why, though. It was because of Chris' ability to focus his intent and create his reality according to his wishes. He is not always able to focus so easily in areas other than work but I have confidence he will master more of this ability with time. As it is, he has taught me a great deal about having a belief in one's own ability to create what one wants in life.

I have used these skills in my own life, even though it seems to come harder for me and I have had to really work at it. It took ten years of unconscious work as well as a year or so of very focused, conscious work to get my family out of the city and move them to a new house in a quiet wooded area forty miles away. When it finally worked out for us, I thought I had only been working at creating it for a few months so I figured I had done pretty well! The house we found was exactly right for us, complete with a pool in the backyard, which had been a part of my vision. We were fortunate enough to find sellers who agreed to a ridiculously low down payment and the loan went through at the bank without a hitch even though Bruce was certain we would run into all sorts of problems. It was a dream come true when we moved in and found ourselves there in a lovely home, far from the harsh realities of city life, able to relax in our pool and listen to the birds singing in the trees above. We could hardly believe it!

A few weeks after we moved into this new house, I was sifting through some boxes when I came across an old journal notebook from about ten years before. As I lifted it out of the box, a clump of magazine clippings fell out of it, landing with a soft rustle on the carpet. I picked these clippings up, sorting through them slowly, my mind in a whirl. I had forgotten these! They were pictures and photos cut out of various magazines, meant to help me visualize my dream home. There was my spacious family room, the roomy kitchen, the deck, and the many bedrooms. Many of the clippings bore a striking resemblance to our new surroundings! One in particular struck me with force. It was a photo of a back yard with a swimming pool and deck surrounded by beautiful trees. A dead ringer for our own back yard! I stuck the picture up on the refrigerator to remind myself of the power to create which lies within us.

When Bruce passed the refrigerator later that day, he stopped and stared.

"Where did you get this?" he asked, pointing at the clipping.

"Out of a magazine," I told him, grinning.

"What? How did a picture of our back yard get into a magazine?"

I laughed because it certainly did look exactly like our own place, complete with the lower level patio doors, the upper deck, the pool, the woods, everything. What an eye opener! But what really hit me was the realization that while I had forgotten about this visualization exercise, putting the clippings away in a notebook, my unconscious mind had been chewing away at this project for more than a decade, trying to bring it into fruition. It was only when my conscious mind got involved that it came about but I am sure that is why it all fell into place so easily; my unconscious self was already in a very supportive position!

I felt I was slow to come to these kinds of revelations in life, late for my awakenings at every turn. Why hadn't I created this beautiful house sooner? Why hadn't I created myself a more prosperous environment years ago? I had been working with spirit for so many years, I didn't understand why some things seemed to take me so long to manifest in my life. With some degree of frustration, I approached Baji with these questions. As always, he pointed out the value of *all* my past experiences, including the hardships.

Baji: Your station in life will depend upon where your soul interest was directed - where you wanted to play out your drama here on the earth plane. A formal education or special training in a specific area will take you into particular arenas where you will have opportunities to learn and grow according to your soul-level intentions. Other scenarios, such as alcoholism or extreme poverty or worldwide fame or overnight success will send you into other arenas. Always, at the core of your being there is choice, choice, choice. It all depends upon where you are interested in playing.

The ability to face and understand Self is the greatest challenge humans face. Seeing the realities of one's self is the most difficult hurdle to overcome in spiritual development. How clear you become in your perceptions of self is how clear you will be in your readings of others, and of your assessments about future possibilities.

The main deterrent for most people in seeing or feeling the magic of life and the power of one's own creative power is FEAR: Fear that they aren't enough somehow, or won't ever be enough. When people are continually afraid of what life will throw at them, they are saying in a sense that they don't believe in their own abilities to handle life. They have no trust in their own higher design, which brought them here in the first place. This kind of thinking makes it difficult, even impossible, to move forward because it blocks creative potential on all sides.

When one is looking out at life with the limitations of an ego perspective, it is natural for that person to experience

159

apprehension - sometimes to the extreme. Ego did not take part in the initial design of your experiences here; it is not able to see things from a spiritual perspective. Thus, Ego is a victim, for it cannot understand the power of spiritual forces. So, even as Ego is a necessary part of the human experience, it is the very thing that must be put aside in order to understand things of a spiritual nature.

To emerge out of fear, it is important to pay attention to the signs and clues and guides that are all around you at every moment. They are everywhere! A bird's chirping, a squirrel running quickly across your path, a loud crash somewhere in the distance, a song coming on the radio... these hints will help you to understand those desires and thoughts that are held at the unconscious level. It is very difficult to create one thing in your life while your unconscious desires are leading you in a completely different direction. Understanding the Self is a necessary part of creating what you want. There will be countless distractions around you each day, and much of what you encounter will seem meaningless to you but pay attention anyway because if something seems to have meaning to you - even for just a split second - then it absolutely does, and you should take note. A constant monitoring of your system is vital, for you have a choice each and every day, each and every moment, as to which direction you will focus your attention.

Only you are able to decide where you will look, what you will listen to, how you will interpret the activities of others. The earth world is full of proof to the contrary when you begin to believe in and follow your own intuition, but if you decide to have a firm trust in Spirit, this negativity will sway you less and less. When you come upon opposing energy, simply send it back to where it came from. You don't need it or want it, so don't take it and hold onto it. As you grow to know your inner self more and more, you will be able to decipher which parts of the outer world you wish to accept and which parts you can leave behind.

Of course, each soul is a universe unto itself and even an entire physical lifetime of work will not reveal all parts of the Self, but the more you do understand, the greater your creative powers will be. One thing to keep in mind is that imagination is just thought. Humans tend to think of imagination as good for them in a creative sense, and this is true, but it can also be a distraction serving to block one from growth, especially when motivated by fears and insecurities. Watch your thoughts, pay attention to what affects you and why, get to know yourself better so that you become more and more aware of what you are creating in your life. What is the world reflecting back at you? Is it negative or positive? Those negative parts will serve to enlighten you to where you need to develop your inner being. Be grateful for the lessons they bring you, accept their teachings and move on.

It is wise to approach others without prejudice, for no matter what they appear to be on the outside, everyone exists with endless possibilities. You never know where your inspiration or profound lessons will come from, or who they will come through.

Each soul has an immense power to create, no matter how weak they appear to be on the surface. Thoughts, feelings, intentions: these are powerful, dynamic forces with definite consequences and when you are involved with others, you are involved with a complex network of emotion and insight. Don't be too quick to judge what you cannot fully see.

Be careful to open your mind to new perspectives; don't get mired down into a single way of looking at something. If you are thinking of a particular issue in just one way, you are missing the benefits and lessons another view might bring. If you are tuned into one reality with no room for others to infringe upon your thoughts, you are keeping yourself at a certain level of illusion and other realities will be invisible to you. Many truths are missed out on because of this. Don't limit yourself. The rewards of an open and inquisitive mind are too great!

One thing I have come to realize is that my creative powers become much stronger in my conscious life when I am content, satisfied, and grateful for exactly where I am in any given moment. The more I learn to find peace and joy in the moment, the easier my desires seem to find their way into fruition. The stronger my focus is in the present, the greater is my power to direct my will at every turn. If I am wasting time dwelling on something in the past, or worrying about the future, my energy is being drained away from the NOW. But if I am able to keep my interest and focus in the present, my energy is much stronger and my creative abilities much more powerful.

It is also easier to catch the habits of self that serve to block creative energies when one is focused in the moment. If you are keeping track of your thoughts, watching how you react to things, taking note of what sort of things affect you, it is much more likely that you will notice when your energy is strong and when it is not. What is depleting your energy? What makes you feel incompetent? These discoveries of self are very important when attempting to manifest visions in your life. Once you become aware of such things, you will be able to change what doesn't serve you well, changing it into creative power. It is not as simple as just telling yourself that you are strong, you are smart, you are capable, etc., although these things are helpful. We must also observe ourselves in our habitual states, learning about our patterns of thought and behavior. If many of our habits are unconscious, they cannot be consciously changed until we become aware of their presence. Asking for assistance from Spirit helps, but we must do the work ourselves as well. We will only change if and when we truly want to - with all parts of our being.

I have found that Spirit helps tremendously in keeping me focused in the moment. Over time, it becomes easier and easier but if I do start to drift into thoughts or behaviors that are useless or harmful to my intention, Spirit will often intervene to get my attention. A book may fall off a shelf for no reason, or my cat will suddenly leap from her chair and race out of the room. These things startle me out of whatever daydream or frame of mind I was in and remind me to focus my attention on what is happening in front of me. The more I do this, the more easily creative work flows forth and the quicker I am able to see the manifestation of my dreams.

We are living in a very temporary state here on earth, with little time to mull over various details if we ever want to get anything done. Consequently, it seems the technique of keeping ourselves within the moment works the best. In the moment, we lose the pressure of our limitations. In the moment, we are free of burdens, future and past, and are able to then focus our intentions toward what is directly in front of us. In a world where time constraints surround everything, this is probably the most powerful way we can operate.

*I am looking for my higher self today
because I need to feel better
I find her there
She was waiting for me to call
She has the right words
She has the insight I am searching for...
I feel better.*

Michelle Senjem and Rebecca LeTourneau

Healing Energy

Hooray, we were going to the beach! Summer had worn on and on, making us weary of our sweaty, sticky skin so when Dad told us he was going to take us to McCarron's Lake for the day we were overjoyed. Eight kids and Vivian piled into the car, squeezing against one another with our towels and tanning oil, as Dad climbed in behind the wheel and started off.

"Oh, look," he said, as we rounded a corner a few blocks away, "I think I need to stop here real quick."

"Oh, John," my mother said, twisting her mouth in annoyance, "you said you would take us to the lake. The kids are hot."

"Yeah, we're boiling," Mark chimed in, and the rest of us clamored in agreement.

"It'll just take a few minutes," Dad said. "I'll be right back."

He had already parked the car and was off to quench his thirst in a small dark bar on the corner. Sighing, the rest of us settled back to wait. Ho hum.

"Well, lookee there," Mom said, pointing. "Looks like Uncle Tom is stopping too."

Our uncle, who had been following behind us with his own family, was already hustling to catch up with my father, his shoulders hunched in embarrassment as we all watched. Irene, my mother's sister who had married Dad's brother Tom, appeared at the window of our car with my two double-cousins Doug and Daryl.

"Well," Mom said, "we might as well sit outside so we don't die of heatstroke in here."

We all clutched and crawled our way out of the sticky seats to lean against the outside of the car in the hot sun. What a disappointment!

"Did you see Tom walking in there?" Mom asked Irene. "He was walking with that East hunch."

Irene laughed. "That's nothing. You should have seen him this morning when I told him the pipes were broken under the sink again. He turned into an instant East cripple."

Mom chortled at the idea of Uncle Tom trying to get out of household chores, and soon the two of them were exchanging stories about the "East men." We kids laughed and laughed at their funny descriptions of our fathers, feeling somewhat vindicated for our mistreatment.

When Dad finally emerged out of the bar, we all climbed back into the vehicle to continue our venture to the beach. Vivian lashed out at him, her voice loud and angry; how dare he make us wait like that? But Dad only laughed at her indignation and stopped at another bar a few blocks further ahead.

"I'll be really fast this time," he promised.

Once again, Irene and Mom propped themselves up against the hood of the car and entertained us with funny stories about the men. By the time Dad and Uncle Tom returned, we all had stomach aches from laughing so hard. Again, our mother yelled and cursed at our father for putting us through such an ordeal, and again he laughed it off. A bit later, he stopped again at another bar. Then another, and another. Each time he disappeared into the grimy little buildings to drink some more beer, Mom and Irene would entertain us until his return, after which time Mom would lay into Dad with a vengeance. By the time we finally reached McCarron's Lake, most of the day had disappeared and we had only a couple of hours left to romp in the water.

Romp we did, though, as my father slept under a tree, and Vivian splashed in the water with us, teasing and chasing her eight children around as if she were a child herself. When Dad woke up, we all had to pile into the car again - in a hurry, too, for he was anxious to drop us off at home and get back to the bar!

This is just one example of how Vivian used humor to lighten the burden that had become our lives. Somehow, she managed to turn everything into a joke and we found ourselves laughing even while enduring troubles and distress. Even though we were poor, she had a way of making us feel as though we had enough and would often joke about our poverty, turning it into a kind of game.

One time, we were moving into a different house and had everything packed in the house, waiting to be hauled onto a moving truck. Vivian had done all of the packing herself and was now relaxing on the porch with the rest of us while Dad left to pick up the rented moving truck. I sat there with my brothers and sister, again in the hot sun, waiting and waiting. Of course, he had gone to the bar again! For hours and hours we sat there, all of our belongings in boxes, waiting for his return.

We did not become too agitated, however, for once again, our mother kept us in stitches as she imitated the old 'Pa Kettle' in her lazy drawl. "Come spring," she kept saying, "I'm gonna have to move." And we would laugh and laugh at the expressions on her face and at the way she hunched over like a lazy East man. We sat there until dark, chuckling on the porch, telling one another, "come spring, we're really gonna have to move."

When I think back to those years of childhood, I am amazed at the healing power of Vivian's humor. It sustained me through countless trials, always giving me a boost just when frustration seemed to be ready to overtake me. I don't believe it a coincidence that I began to slide further and further down a road of lonely desperation at about the same time I became more and more estranged from my mother. We fought during my teen years, mostly because she was so worried about me and I was intent upon my own, quite destructive, path. But without her easy laughter in my ears, the lighter side of life disappeared and I was left with the hollow realities of life without joy.

Like Vivian, my husband Bruce kept me in stitches even while infuriating me with his drinking. It took him years to quit, years to put it behind him and become the wonderful, sober man he is today. But bitterness wasn't able to take root between us during those early years because of the healing power of laughter. We were always able to come back to laughter, even after the worst of arguments. Laughter is what tied us together, what helped us to maintain our connection and what gave us memories to treasure even though there were hard times mixed in there, too. Now that we have managed to overcome those problems and find ourselves the best of friends, laughter remains one of the main ingredients of our relationship. I believe there is little else that heals the way laughter does.

It wasn't so long ago that my brother Mark was dying of cancer. This is the reality we were faced with as he went in for surgery one morning. It all happened so quickly that none of us in the family were able to be there since he was far away in Seattle and hadn't had much warning ahead of time. I was beside myself with worry. He was so talented, so young - how could he die so soon? I knew there was a chance he would survive and I wanted to send all the healing energy I could toward him but it was difficult to keep my thoughts away from troubling doubts and anxiety. As the morning wore on, I paced through the house, unable to concentrate on anything productive.

The doorbell rang as I was pacing and I opened it to find Patty standing there, a wide grin on her face. She had just been in the neighborhood, she said, and wanted to pop in for a few minutes. The light in her eyes revealed her good mood and I couldn't help but laugh at the way she stood so straight and proper, holding a paper bag in one hand.

"I brought you a gift," she said, primly. There were cinnamon rolls in the bag, fresh from the bakery, and we sat down in the kitchen with some coffee, enjoying the sweet taste.

Patty, who is usually alive with jokes and laughter, was no different on that morning. She had recently been spotting 'trolls' in the real world, she said, and was describing some of these episodes. I rocked with laughter as she imitated a woman at work who tried so hard to be sophisticated only to sabotage herself by creating the most unlikely messes. Patty is a wonderful imitator of trolls. She says they are all around us and not too hard to spot if you only look. They try to pass themselves off as regular humans but don't do a very good job of it. It doesn't matter what they look like either: beautiful or ugly, tall or short, fat or thin - a troll can come in any shape or size. What gives away a troll is trollish behavior – which can invade any of us if we aren't careful, and this was what Patty was imitating as I held my shaking sides.

About two hours later, while wiping tears of laughter from my eyes, I fought to regain control of my senses enough to answer the phone. It was Mark's ex-wife calling to tell me they had just wheeled him out of surgery.

"It took two hours," she said, "not too bad. They think it went really well, too."

I was very relieved to hear this, feeling an immediate sense of hope for Mark's future. When I told Patty about it, she was concerned she had distracted me from thinking about him during his surgery.

"I know you wanted to concentrate and focus your energy," she said, apologetically.

But I told her our two hours of laughing together was the best medicine I could have imparted to my brother. Because I was able to keep myself in such a lighthearted place for those two hours, I was able to send my unconscious anxieties out the window, sending energy of love and happiness to my brother. He was never far from my thoughts but the joking and laughing created a frame of mind to hold this concern in so that it wouldn't become swallowed up in useless anxiety.

Laughter heals, this I believe. And laughter also fuels good and strong energy, helping one to support another in time of need. I didn't know Mark went into surgery that morning at that time; I only knew it was going to be some time that day. I also had no idea that he would be wheeled out of surgery just as Patty was preparing to walk out the door! She had no plans to visit me that day and had come on a whim. I had asked for help in sending my brother positive energy so that he would be strong for surgery and everything would go well.

Since I don't believe in coincidence, I am quite sure that Patty was sent to me, or perhaps heard my call of need at some level, and appeared as an angel of support with her laughter. She kept me in a state of amusement for the two hours Mark was in surgery and then she left. It was exactly what I needed. It was the most I could do for Mark at that time, that day, that hour. He came through the surgery with flying colors and went on to recover from the cancer, going into a long remission that he is still enjoying today. I know he is on his own path and his cancer probably has little to do with me but because he is my brother and I love him, I give him whatever energy support I can to make his road easier. That day, when he was under the knife and his future was very uncertain, I knew he needed all the support he could get so I prayed and meditated, sending him all the healing energies I could muster. But I really feel that Patty's visit is what enabled me to send him the best gift of all - the healing power of laughter.

I really think Patty was a court jester in a former life. She has this innate ability to find the funny side to just about everything and continually leaves people in stitches behind her wherever she goes. It is amazing that she can face life with such good humor after all the horrors she has experienced over the years but much like my mother, laughter has been her saving grace. She actually has nicknames for some of those who hurt her during childhood and throws them into stories in which their human shortcomings are laid wide open. She jokes her way through financial problems, marital annoyances, and work-related stresses. She jumps in elevators at just the right moment so that her head will almost brush the ceiling. She turns a leaky tent in the rain into a hilarious game of dodge-the-drops and patch-the-holes wherein everyone is screaming with laughter. Children love her, clamoring for her attention wherever she goes.

Sure, there are times when she feels irritated or depressed but Patty's natural state of being is always very close to laughter. Some people are just like that. And, if you think about it, they are magical to be around. By the sheer force of their humorous energy, they can transform an entire room of people into a resounding concert of mirth. Their easy and genuine chuckles, giggles, and belly laughter serve as a gift - a healing and uplifting gift - that benefits all who come their way.

It's interesting to me that I happened to meet Patty during my troubled teen years after I had detached so much from my mother. What drew me to Patty was her wacky sense of humor, so constant it sometimes bordered on insanity. Obviously, I was missing this element of laughter in my life since Vivian was no longer playing a central role in my drama so I proceeded to replace her with Patty's friendship. The two of us spent our time together giggling uncontrollably as one joke after another rolled out of us. It got to be so obnoxious to our friends they wouldn't allow us to ride in the same car together when going out to party.

"No way," they would say, blocking us at the car door, "only one of you can get in here. The other has to ride in the other car."

But our laughter and joking, while sometimes irritating to our friends, served to bond Patty and I in a very unique way. For one thing, we had come from similar backgrounds so we understood the importance of humor in impossible situations. We could poke fun at our pasts because we each knew the other had full knowledge of the pain involved - this was not necessary to describe. So the laughing came easy as we each attempted to distance ourselves from our childhoods. Without the mirth and the frivolity, we would have been soaked in tears after what we had been through. Laughing our way out of it was much more enjoyable.

We lost touch as we got older, drifting off in different directions, but many years later we were to find each other again.

Bruce and I had recently moved into our new home and I was feeling quite lonely for good company. I had many friends but none who supplied me with that wonderful sense of humor that was Patty's natural gift. I missed her. Likewise, she was in a lonely period, having recently gained her sobriety. She had left all of her partying friends behind and was venturing forth on a quieter path where not so many people were clamoring after her. One day, she looked up my number and called me - after years of not talking to one another. Imagine our surprise when we discovered we lived only five miles apart!

It was the most natural thing in the world to pick up our friendship exactly where we had left it, joking and laughing our way into one another's hearts and lives again. Not long after our reunion, Patty was placed in my school to work - right in my office with me! We thoroughly enjoyed our time together there as we created a lighthearted atmosphere of fun and laughter that affected everyone who came near us. When Patty left, some years later, her humorous ways and cheery comments were sorely missed by the entire staff.

Baji: Spiritually speaking, most things have an element of humor to them, especially within the human realm. From the energy of an ever-changing human drama, things look a bit different from the perspective of spirit - not so permanent, you see. This takes away the painful aspects that are so very real and so very strongly felt at the human level. Spirit is looking always from a broader perspective, and sees meaning and love and yes, humor, where humans may not be aware of these things.

A powerful movement of energy occurs whenever you let go and enjoy a moment. Laughter can also serve as a reminder of the worthwhile nature of life's blunders, keeping one lighter and more responsive to the higher frequencies of thought and creation.

Not so very long ago, there was this beautiful, white, longhaired bundle of a kitten lying on a fallen tree just beyond our back yard, looking up at me through my bedroom window. Her black tail was in sharp contrast to the rest of her, as was one black ear that twitched back and forth as she regarded me with curiosity. I had seen her before, about a month earlier, when she had been lying on that same log with her mother and two fluffy siblings. I had decided to bring them food, seeing as they were obviously wild and depending on their wits in the woody patches of the neighborhood. They seemed to thoroughly enjoy my offerings for a few days but then all at once they were gone, and the dish of food I put out for them remained untouched. I didn't know if I would ever see them again. I figured the Fourth of July fireworks might have caused them to search for a more peaceful home somewhere else. Couldn't blame them really; I don't like the noise of the fireworks either. But I missed them, my little wild friends, and prayed that life would provide what they needed.

And now, here she was again, the little one with the black tail, right there on that fallen tree, her eyes glittering in the sunlight as she watched me. Pleased and excited, I hurried downstairs and made my way through the brush toward the dog-size kennel I had left near the woods. Of course they would come back, I thought. Who else was going to put food out for them and provide shelter from the storms? No matter that they ran whenever I came near, that was to be expected. They were wild after all. I knew they didn't run too far, just enough to disguise themselves among the thick branches and leaves until I had filled their dishes and turned back toward the house.

However, this time the little kitten on the log did not run when I bent to fill the dish with cat food. She sat very still, watching me. What was this? Had this one decided to give up the wildwoods life and become my pet? I took a step closer to her, then another. Slowly, slowly I advanced until something told me

175

to stop about three feet away. I waited, watching her intently, wondering what had made me stop since she had not yet run off.

As our eyes met, so close, I was shocked clear through to my bones to see in her gaze a look that does not belong in a small kitten's eyes. A dreadful, painful look, one of knowing the worst of pain. I had seen that look before, in my own mirror, on my own face long ago. I knew that same searing agony which was penetrating that kitten's body, keeping her still on that log.

Even while this horrible comprehension was flooding through me, the kitten lifted her head and turned it slowly, revealing a wound so hideous I burst into tears. Her neck had been slashed open, numerous slices across a hugely swollen neck, and pus I knew instantly was poisonous dripped onto her clotted fur along with the blood. She was dying right in front of my eyes. Why had she come back to show me her death? Why did I have to witness the brutality of nature, the effects of a vicious attack on my sweet little friend by some other wild creature? What was the sense in it when all I wanted to do was to love and care for these beautiful animals?

Sobbing, I moved forward to scoop her up, only to have her vanish quickly into the thick brush surrounding us. After waiting for a while, there was nothing left for me to do but go back into the house and wonder at what I had just seen. What was I supposed to do? I felt very strongly that the little kitten had come to me for help but how could I help her when she wouldn't let me near enough to touch her?

As I paced back and forth in my kitchen, trying to figure out what to do, the phone rang and I picked it up to hear my son's lovely voice in my ear. Immediately, he demanded to know what was wrong. Far away at boot camp in Michigan, he had sensed my distress and felt moved to call me right away. My voice shaking with emotion, I told him about the injured kitten and how it wouldn't let me near enough to help it.

"I don't know what to do," I told him.

"Well, have you been praying for it?" he asked.

I was surprised at this, for usually praying would have been one of my first reactions to this kind of trouble. But I hadn't been thinking clearly at all, too wrapped up in my own inadequacies to concentrate on spirit help.

"No," I admitted, "but I will now."

Chris talked to me a bit longer, his calm assurance comforting me greatly. How wonderful to have his love and support so near even when he was so far away! When I hung up, I hurried into my room to pray for the tiny kitten, glad my son had the sense to see what I had been too worked up to look at. With heartfelt sincerity I prayed for the healing of that little white being outside. I felt the presence of spirit around me then, filling me with that familiar warmth and comfort. Afterward, I sat very still for a few moments, waiting for direction.

Suddenly I remembered my own pain of the past week, when an infected tooth sent me into agony for days. For hours I laid in bed, a heavy throbbing in my jaw, my tongue thick and heavy, my throat burning with pain every time I swallowed. The antibiotics the dentist had given me were supposed to clear everything up in about ten days so I clung to this hope as I curled up under the covers, shivering against the pain. It had been so bad that I insisted my dentist give me a double dosage of antibiotics, twenty days instead of ten, but my fears had been unfounded. By the time the first ten days were up, my throat had gone back to its normal size and the infection had slipped away, leaving my jaw and tongue intact. How good it was to feel no pain! But now I felt that I must have gone through that agonizing time so I would know the experience of this little white bundle outside. I could already feel my throat tightening up again, could feel the deep gash across my neck. Why did I have to know the pain of this kitten? What good did it do to understand it if I couldn't do anything to relieve it?

When my sixteen-year-old daughter Jill emerged from her vampire cave of a bedroom in the basement a bit later in the day, she found me crying on the sofa. I knew I was to be learning a lesson from all this but sometimes the lessons are so painful!

"What's wrong?" she asked, startled. I told her about the kitten, knowing that she had watched it affectionately from the window many times just as I had. A tortured look came over her face as I described the ugly wound.

"We have to do something," she said, her voice filled with urgency. I agreed, but admitted I didn't know quite what to do.

"I asked for spirit help," I told her, "and I know this is a learning experience for me. But I'm not content with that. I have to do something to help that beautiful little angel!"

"Yes, you do," Jill agreed. We decided we needed expert advice so together we called every animal support number we could find in the phone book. However, living in a rural community, we found very few choices for animal rescue and soon realized that there would be no help for that poor wild kitten out there unless it came from us. Jill felt sorry for me because of all my crying and because of my recent toothache that had kept me in bed for so many desperate hours the week before. Usually on my last nerve, she suddenly became very nurturing and concerned, fussing over me like a mother hen. Funny thing about teenagers, just when you think they have completely lost their minds and all sense of reason, they turn right around and act more mature than their parents. I was really confused.

"You're still taking those antibiotics, aren't you?" she asked, patting my shoulder as I hung up the phone in discouragement. I wiped my eyes, shaking my head in sorrow. Then suddenly a thought struck me. Could it possibly help...? I thought of that awful, gaping wound in the poor creature's neck and wondered... but decided it was worth a try. Antibiotics could do wonders sometimes, right? I broke open the red capsule and sprinkled the white powder into a can of tuna and rushed it down to the spot near the fallen tree. Sure enough, she was there again, this time with her mother and two white siblings. I set the can down and sent visual images to the mother, concentrating until I felt she understood the importance of the contents within this particular meal.

Back in my bedroom, I watched as the injured kitten ate the tuna while her siblings played with one another nearby. The mother sat very still, watching me with wary but grateful eyes, her gaze never wavering from mine until the tiny one had finished taking her medicine. For ten days I repeated my antibiotic-tuna run. By day nine, I was watching in amazement as the once dying kitten played with her black tail and chased flies, her energy returning with a vengeance. Now, when I ventured near, she ran away as fast as the others. Never had I been so glad to see her race away from me in that skittish fervor. They all disappeared again on the eleventh day. I chuckled when I realized the ten-day dosage the dentist had prescribed for me had been just the right amount for the kitten also!

I learned so much from that little injured kitten, especially about faith. As I pursue my own spiritual growth, I am learning to expect life's grace even as I am forced to face lingering fears and painful moments. Now, when I think of my furry little friend, there is no burning or swollen pain in my throat. Instead, I feel a slight itch on my neck from the loss of hair, and the healing.

Baji: This was a very interesting scenario Michelle planted into her life. She has always been interested in healing work and, as a result, is continuously placing herself into positions where her healing powers will be developed. In this case, she was not able to place hands on the kitten and transmit energy this way, so she had to come up with a creative solution. She tried sending the healing energy through the power of her mind, but this didn't seem to be doing the trick.

This could have done the trick, really, but she was intent upon learning a different lesson this time around. The thing is, sometimes miracles will come in the most practical way imaginable. The fact that Michelle used the antibiotics her dentist gave her was a very concrete physical thing to do, but it encouraged spiritual growth on many levels. For one thing, the synchronicity of her own toothache pain and the kitten's injury, along with their mutual need for medicine, served to prove how much her creative powers were at work even before she was aware of it.

Also, the idea of using the antibiotics came to her after meditation and prayer, reinforcing her commitment to follow such methods in the future.

Prayer always helps me to feel closer to Spirit. It elevates my energy levels and intensifies my focus so that my creative intentions gain momentum and power. It is a way of connecting to my Higher Self, to the other dimensions of my soul, to my Spirit-Circle, to God. I recognize the Divinity within myself when I pray. It is a wonderful, all-encompassing feeling of joy to sense the Divine Nature within oneself, which is why I pray so often.

Generally, prayer can be engaged in at any time, anywhere. All that is needed is thought and intention. Sometimes, I am praying as I drive, shop, or do household chores. Sometimes, I am praying while talking or listening to someone. Other times, I go into a room alone, making sure I will not be distracted by anyone, and immerse myself in a prayerful meditation. During these sessions I am usually intensely focused on something extremely important to me at the time. Often, I am sending someone healing energies, or will stop periodically in order to listen for messages from Spirit.

Some people feel more comfortable combining ritual with prayer, thinking it makes the whole exercise more meaningful. Personally, I feel that the prayer itself, being heartfelt and intensely directed energy, is all that is required to bring about change or direction. But this is not to say that rituals are not helpful and are not appreciated by Spirit, because I am positive they are. Rituals are also a most helpful way to connect your unconscious mind to what you are consciously praying about.

But the prayer itself is the main thing. Prayer is the energy that can move mountains, dry up oceans, open hearts and minds, stop a war, heal a child, lift a sorrow and comfort a soul. Prayer is divine energy in motion. We have this energy at our disposal each and every moment - so why don't we use it more often?

Baji: You have tremendous power for healing yourselves and others. It requires a trust in Self and a strength that comes from an inner knowing, enabling one to see beyond what appears to be. Sometimes, an illness or difficult situation has not outworn its usefulness to the soul plan and so will not be easily subject to healing, while at other times, the very event is merely a vehicle through which one was meant to learn about the healing powers within.

One thing that can block healing, as well as many other things, is fear. Fear of the illness itself may be stronger than one's trust in his or her own spiritual depth. Fear of growth is another possibility, or fear of facing certain aspects of oneself. Also, a difficult situation may sometimes turn out to be a blessing, for it might well serve to propel someone ever faster toward his or her authentic desires. Usually this type of situation can only be seen for what it is after the fact, when one looks back and sees the pattern from a different perspective.

At other times, especially when the healing is directed at another, it may be that this person has other plans than to be healed at that time. If this is true, then no matter what you do, the healing will not take place. Whatever the situation, your power to heal is only as strong as the conviction of your trust and intention, as well as the trust and intentions of those who are asking for healing.

Sometimes, these things are in alignment with one another and a seemingly miraculous healing will take place. This is due to an agreement between the healer and the injured party, even if this agreement takes place at an unconscious level. When things are in alignment, magic happens! When things are not so much in alignment, however, healing might not take place so quickly.

Still, one can always strive toward bringing him or herself into alignment with healing power. As with anything positive, this takes a certain amount of understanding of the motives and desires and fears of Self. Healing powers come from the same place all powers come from: deep within the inner being that is always rooted in Spirit.

I have learned that listening to our bodies is perhaps the most important part of healing work. This is true when you are trying to heal yourself, and also when attempting to help others who are in pain. Usually, if I am around someone who is suffering some kind of physical ailment, I will feel a slight pain in similar regions of my own body. This becomes significantly more intense if I touch that person and focus my thoughts on the affected area. Sometimes, I will sense that there is something a person is not looking at in his or her life, something they are avoiding at all costs. This may be an emotional issue or a physical one. For instance, it may be at times that the person simply needs to cut a bad habit such as smoking out of his or her life, or needs to be exercising or eating different foods. Yet even when this is true, there is usually an emotional issue of some kind behind the bad habit that is asking for release.

It is not always easy to heal myself when suffering from some kind of illness but I am always certain that there is a lesson in there somewhere, trying to get my attention. From the instant I begin feeling sick, I am looking for the answer. Sometimes it isn't so hard to find, other times it is more elusive and I may not understand it until days or weeks later. But it is surely true that our illnesses are messages to us - there is something within ourselves to which we should be paying attention. The fact that we agreed to come here and experience the physical plane indicates we also agreed to participate in various ailments to one degree or another, so I do not view such afflictions as entirely negative; obviously much is learned through these experiences.

But I also believe we are discovering new and miraculous things about the power of healing with all our many experiments, so our willingness to endure such pain is a testament to our dedication toward a richer understanding of all of life. We are a brave and courageous bunch who have volunteered to spend some time here in this dimension! Even though things may get tough and we may get very discouraged, we should always remember that our time here, our experiences here - including our physical suffering - is valued and appreciated by all the realms and dimensions of life.

Through various experiences, I have learned much about the guidance received from body. Now, whenever I feel myself becoming ill or off-balance, I immediately stop and tune in. No matter which part of my body is hurting, it will have a message for me, something it wants me to look at. Repressed memories are one possible reason a body will react negatively but there can be many other reasons as well. Maybe a drastic shift in focus is needed, or a particular insight into a certain situation is begging for attention. Maybe the ailment will lead one into asking for help in a way that will set an entirely new adventure in motion.

Whatever the reasons for sickness or discomfort, however, our bodies can reveal volumes of what we don't know. To tune into its wisdom we must be open to what comes. We must be willing to accept the information we receive with honesty and gratitude. Our intention must be to journey toward truth, whatever the consequences, no matter how difficult it is to face. This takes patience and courage and a commitment to the journey of one's soul. Sometimes, the issues that arise are terribly frightening or uncomfortable. Sometimes, we can feel entirely too weary to continue as we struggle through physical pain. But we do have a loving support around us at all times, and insights *will* come. Doors, windows, skies, and hearts will burst open to reveal a whole new world.

Trust your body, your cells, your precious physical gift of human life. Listen to its wisdom. Be patient with the process, accept the adventure as it plays out, and watch your beautiful Spirit unfold. I can tell you from personal experience it is well worth the effort!

Sometimes, no matter what we do or how much we want it, a healing does not take place and we are forced to deal with the pain of losing someone to physical death. This is incredibly difficult to endure, for we know that we will no longer be able to look at that loved one's face or hear their voice or feel their warm touch as long as we are here on earth. At least we won't see them *physically*, and this is hard to take.

Before my father died, he lapsed into a coma that lasted for two weeks. The last time I saw him, I stood next to him, rubbing his arthritic fingers the way I used to before he got so sick. It was my turn to sit with him; all of my siblings had been there at various times, sitting with him even though he could no longer speak to us or even motion with his eyes. The doctor had been in a while earlier, informing me that if my father was taken off the ventilator he would surely die that evening. His breathing was already very labored and his heart would stop without the help of the ventilator.

"He's not afraid to die," I said, in my strongest voice, "but he is afraid of living on like this, hooked up to machines that will only prolong the inevitable."

I knew my father felt this way because he had confessed it to my mother a few weeks earlier. Even though she was now married to someone else, he confided his worst fears to her, knowing she was the one person in the world who would understand.

A nurse walked in the room as I stood there stroking my father's hand. She threw a sympathetic glance my way and apologized for having to interrupt me.

"I have to give him his treatment," she said. By this, I knew she meant she had to pound on his chest to loosen the fluids in his lungs - something I hated to watch. Reluctantly, I placed my father's limp hand back on the bed and took a step back, but then froze in amazement as he suddenly reached up and grabbed my fingers! I gasped in surprise, leaning forward to gaze down at his quiet face. The nurse gasped, too, staring at me in disbelief.

"Look at that," she whispered, eyes wide.

"Dad? Dad, I'm here, I'm here," I said, tears slipping down my cheeks. I told him I loved him so, so much and that I would never forget all the love he had shown me in my life. I could feel that he was already hurting about many of the things he had put his children through and I wanted him to feel forgiveness from me and unconditional love so that he would feel free to pass on. Still, with all my yearning, he did not open his eyes. I was glad the nurse had seen him grab my hand so tightly, knowing it would not be easy for others to believe he had done such a thing. He died a few hours later, as all his children hurried to his side.

The death of my dear father served to propel me forward with a great force as I sought spiritual understanding of death. Why do people we love have to be taken from us? As I searched for answers, I also strove to make a psychic connection with my father in the after world. Soon, he began to visit me in my dreams, talking to me about a great many things. He continually assured me of his presence, telling me that he would be around to guide me as long as I lived in this earthly realm. After some time passed, I began to notice that I could hear his voice while awake as he spoke gently into my ear. Many times, he has alerted me to some kind of distress my mother is going through, enabling me to contact her and offer my help even though she wouldn't have asked for it. Other times he has directed a question at one of my siblings through me, which will send them

Michelle Senjem and Rebecca LeTourneau

into deep sobs as they recognize that his presence is still around. The most incredible joy for me is that, although I always knew there was that sweet, loving side to John East, now that he has crossed over, he knows it, too.

On a very human level, I hate death. I hate that children die, that loved ones die and that people suffer. I grieve for those who have lost loved ones, especially children, for there is nothing worse, in my view, that one can go through in the earth realm than losing a child. However, when I am strongly immersed in Spirit, I can see death from a different perspective, which calms me immensely. It helps to realize that this situation is temporary, that we will certainly be reunited with our loved ones again. And it helps to know that each death is a profound event, serving to teach many, many things at many, many levels. Once we return to the spiritual realm we will no longer be bound by our earthly perspective and will see things as decidedly more interesting than we do now. We will no longer be blocked by the painful emotions that swirl through us in the human state.

Viewing various deaths from the spirit realm will be an exciting and eye-opening exercise as we review the many ways people choose to exit this world - and the effects that came after.

The Bond Between Things

Where there is no ground a leaf falls softly
In air and in arms
and legs it falls from atop a lofty tree,
from the summer that yields many lovers and lost healers —
breaking in the morning blues, jumping in a smile, the late night
call has called from nowhere
and somewhere the feisty wind
carries a leaf as it carries
the world.

— Mike East

Michelle Senjem and Rebecca LeTourneau

Gifts in Strange Places

Lola Dane swept into my house, yards and yards of rayon and silk swirling about her wrists and ankles as she brushed past me and stood, eyes closed, in the middle of the living room.

"Hello," I said, a little taken aback by her behavior. But she was not about to answer me; she had something more important to do like check out the energy level of my home or something. I watched her, determined to keep an open mind. Two of my Stillwater friends had insisted I meet this woman, Lola Dane, psychic extraordinaire, and I had finally agreed since they seemed unable to rest until I did. Clarice, one of these friends, stood near the edge of the room looking at me excitedly. Linda, the other friend, had not shown up yet.

Lola lifted her arms, eyes still closed, and began to hum in a monotone voice. Ummmmm. Ummmmm. Ummmmm. Clarice drew in a sharp breath, her hands clasped together at her waist. I stood, silently waiting and watching. Baji? I summoned him with my thoughts. Baji, what is she doing? But there was no sound in the room except her monotone humming. I pictured bees flying out of her mouth and tensed up a bit, feeling an urge to flee. Finally, though, she stopped and opened her eyes.

"I sense pain," she said in a throaty voice. She swept one of her arms through the air in a wide arc. "Right here in this room I sense a great deal of pain."

She looked at me through narrowed eyes.

"Have you been sick?"

"Uh... no."

"Oh yes, Michelle, remember that headache you were complaining about last week?" Clarice broke in, anxiously.

"That's right," I said, snapping my fingers, "I did have a headache that one day."

"I thought it was something to do with the head area," Lola stated loudly. "There are strong vibrations just above your forehead there. I'll bet it was right between your eyes."

"I haven't had headaches for a long time," I said, evasively, "but that one last week was a doozy."

I didn't tell her it had been a pounding one located at the back of my skull, nowhere near my eyes. No need to be rude, I thought. Besides, judging from the relieved smile on Clarice's face, this meeting with Lola was really important to her so I didn't want to ruin things.

"Anyone for coffee?" I asked, inviting them into the kitchen. The two women followed me, Clarice silently thrilled, Lola sniffing in an investigative manner. I hoped she wasn't allergic to cats.

We sat around the kitchen table with our steaming mugs, looking out the patio doors at the wooded area behind my house. The sun was shining, the sky was blue... I resisted an urge to jump up and go for a walk out there in the splendor of the day.

"So," Lola said suddenly, slamming the palm of her hand against the table top, "how long have you known about the gift?"

I jumped. "Uh... the gift?"

My mind raced, thinking of my birthday, which had gone by not long before. Had she and Clarice cooked up a present for me? Was there a surprise in store?

"Michelle has always been psychic," Clarice said, proudly. I nodded with recognition then, realizing this Lola person was referring to psychic ability.

"Well," I said, carefully, "I don't know that I've ever thought about it quite like a gift. More like a developed ability, I guess. I mean, everyone has the same capabilities I do when it comes to connecting with spirit."

"Hogwash," Lola retorted. She leaned back in her chair and sighed a deep, impatient sigh. "Obviously, you are hiding from your mission."

"My mission?"

"Yes. What are you doing at that school? Anyone can work at a school. You have psychic powers, why aren't you using them? You should be doing readings full time."

I stared at her, then at Clarice who had raised her eyebrows in surprise but was saying nothing. Again, I willed myself to be patient and to keep my mind open.

"I created that job at the school," I said, quietly, "and it's very useful work. I feel I am using my abilities, psychic and otherwise, every day of my life."

"But you should be doing readings," Lola snapped. She narrowed her eyes again. "There is a tall dark man standing behind you and he looks very angry. What? What?"

She leaned forward, squinting. I leaned back away from her, a little bit startled.

"Oh, okay," she said, "he says he is your guide Lambert. He says he has already been trying to tell you that you are supposed to be doing readings instead of working at the school."

"That's funny," I said, "I don't feel anything behind me." I didn't mention the fact that I'd never met anyone, spirit or physical, named Lambert.

"Her main guide is Baji," Clarice said, quickly, "he is an Indian guide."

"I said he was dark, didn't I?" snapped Lola. "Of course he's Indian. That's why there is a feather in his hair. Maybe he didn't say Lambert... I was kind of confused about that anyway. But I don't think his name is Baji either. I think it's something like...What? What?"

She frowned, squinting her eyes so much they were almost closed as she glared into the space over my left shoulder.

"Oh," she said, finally sitting back, "he said his name is The Sea."

"The Sea?"

"Yeah. Maybe it's a Native American thing."

I sighed, not willing to tell her Baji appeared to me as an *eastern* Indian when he did appear in human form. Not that he

191

was from India or anything; this is just the image he has chosen to present to me since childhood, knowing I would be comforted by it. I never thought it mattered all that much what form he showed up in because he wasn't physical, he was spirit. But the fact that Lola was talking about a Native American Indian only served to prove that she was grasping at straws, which is what I figured all along - ever since the headache thing, which she had probably heard before from Clarice or Linda anyway.

"That's so cool -" Clarice began, but Lola cut her off with a snap of her wrist through the air.

"Quiet," she snapped, "I'm focusing on Michelle's energy."

Focus she did, too, grabbing my head in both her hands and pushing it one way, then another. I sat there, wondering why I was allowing this strange woman to play with my head like it was play-dough when she suddenly let go, fell back in her chair, and went rigid.

"Oh oh," she moaned, "I'm getting a message, I'm getting a message, I'm getting a message..."

Clarice stared at her with wide eyes. I touched my hair, gingerly, to make sure Lola had not squeezed it all off.

"Yes, yes, you are supposed to quit your job," she said, triumphantly, "...TOMORROW!!! You are supposed to do readings again, full time, RIGHT AWAY!"

"Uh-huh," I murmured. I took a deep breath and held it in for a moment, trying to calm myself. The way she was looking at me with that hard glare made me want to tell her how wrong she was and denounce her as a phony right there on the spot. And me, always so upset with those who do judge practicing psychics so quickly and harshly! But then the doorbell rang.

"I could feel someone coming," Lola said, right away. I ignored her and went to answer the door.

"Did I miss anything?" Linda asked, breathlessly. She hurried into the kitchen behind me, her breath hot on my neck.

"We're just sitting here having some coffee," I told her, "you want some?"

Linda settled in at the table with the rest of us and we resumed our conversation, which had now turned to angels. Thankfully, my defensive feelings of a moment ago had passed and I was able to center myself within the realms of patience once again. As Lola rambled on about the many angels who worked miracles in her everyday life, I silently called upon Baji for help. What was I supposed to be learning from this exchange? I relaxed my mind, letting the others chatter amongst themselves, and drifted into a meditative state right there at the table.

All at once, things became very clear to me. My senses were heightened and I could feel the energy in the room. I could also hear and smell and see at a very intense level as I breathed in the aroma of the coffee mingled with the perfumed scents of the women around my table. I focused my attention on Lola Dane, psychic extraordinaire, and immediately saw her as a very sad and lonely woman, afraid of her own shadow. My heart went out to her because she was holding people at arm's length with the very behavior that attracted them to her. With all her airs and flowing clothes and narrowed eyes, she was disguising who she really was, terrified that her natural state of being was completely unlovable.

As I absorbed this information about Lola and felt compassion for her, a light being appeared behind her head. Instantly, gratitude filled my being for I knew I now had the help and guidance I needed to relate to her.

"Are you artistic in some way?" I asked her, blurting out my question in the middle of her sentence. She stopped talking and stared at me, surprised.

"What?"

"Artistic," I repeated, "do you do some kind of artistic work?"

"I paint," she said, "but not as much anymore."

"Why not?"

"Well, because I'm too busy," she replied, impatiently. "Do you know how many readings I do in a day? Who has time to play around with paints?"

"I didn't know you painted," Clarice said.

"Me either," Linda said, looking at Lola with some surprise. "How come you never showed us any of your work?"

"That's not what my life is about right now," Lola replied, haughtily. She turned to me and sniffed dismissively. "You are really picking up the distant past, Michelle. Tsk, tsk. See how out of touch you are?"

But I understood, then, why she was so angry with me for not doing readings full time. How dare I pursue another avenue of expression when I was able to do readings? For, here she was burdened with her own state of affairs, yearning to paint but feeling compelled to do readings because of guilt or fear or some such thing.

"But maybe painting is something you need to look at again," I told her, gently. "Maybe there is something you need to express through your art. Doing readings isn't the only way to reach people, you know."

"I know that," she snapped, waving a hand at me, "but a gift is a gift and I am not about to turn *my* back on it!"

"Your ability to paint is a gift, too," I said, unruffled by her hostility. She insisted it wasn't the same thing but I saw a flash of hope deep in her eyes and felt the seed had been planted. I wasn't about to change her way of thinking that day, since her blocks were firmly in place and the wall she had built around herself was very high indeed. But I was sure that, with the help of that light being behind her, Lola had been infected with the germ of her own longing. I hoped it would grow and fester until she could no longer ignore it because her gift to the world was obviously meant to include more than psychic readings. I had no doubt that her art work was impressive, for it was her natural calling, and I knew if she were to reopen that part of her soul, her life would change drastically.

There was no reason for me to try and influence her further, so I let it be. We chatted about various things but did not approach the subject of readings again. I noticed Lola stopped attacking me about my job at the school after I mentioned her painting, though. This helped the rest of the visit go smoothly and by the time the three women left, we had created an atmosphere of pleasant friendliness in which to say our good-byes. I knew Lola Dane and I would not soon become fast friends or anything but I was grateful for her visit, as I had learned a great deal. I had been reminded of the importance of following one's true nature, of seeking out our individual bliss, responding to the call of our own spirit.

When these things are ignored, a life will disintegrate into unhappiness and fear, no matter how successful we appear to be on the outside. Lola Dane might be known as psychic extraordinaire, and she certainly did put on a good show, but I would not have traded places with her for anything in the world. Nothing compares to a true connection to spirit. Nothing else can fulfill that part of us which yearns for authentic being. My own path, which was much more ordinary-looking on the outside, was more closely in alignment with the true intentions of my spirit than Lola's was, I was certain of it. Her thoughts could change, she could open up her mind at any moment and let the true guidance of her spirit family in - and I hoped for her sake she would. But for everything there is a time and reason and her time of awakening was not yet.

I was reminded later, through a session with Baji, that I had been quite late myself in recognizing my connection to spirit. It wasn't until many years of destructive behavior nearly killed me that I finally woke up to my intended path. So, there was no reason to judge, or to feel superior to Lola. She was involved in different lessons in a different way, consumed with her own interests. Whatever she chose to do would end up benefiting her at some level in some way.

I was extremely grateful for this lesson as I thought about what my life would be like without being conscious of Spirit, and without being changed by these influences in my life. There was a profound sense of relief in realizing it is entirely possible to live through an entire lifetime without tuning into this extraordinary guidance at all – and I was sure I had lived lifetimes like that before, which made me doubly glad I was only *late* for my plane of spirit consciousness this time around instead of missing the ride altogether.

Maybe I had been slow to get there even in this physical adventure and for sure I had a long way to go, but at least I had finally taken off!

Baji has often spoken to me about the many ways Spirit will work through other people, sometimes in a most bizarre manner, and I know this is true. There was a man once, an old, rough-looking character who sat down at the table next to Bruce, Chris and me at a restaurant. I had been in a tizzy about Jill, worrying incessantly about her behavior in school and her increasingly defiant attitude. All my attempts to contact spirit help had only confused me further as I tried to figure out what to do about her. Should I be more strict? Should I spy on her? Should I just let her do whatever she wanted? It seemed the questions of parenting a wayward teen were just too overwhelming for my state of mind. Those in my Spirit Circle continually sent me comfort and assurance, but I could not maintain any sense of calm, for each day seemed to bring with it a new problem so far as Jill was concerned.

"Mom," Chris said, nodding toward the old man at the next table, "he's talking to you."

"Hmm?"

I turned to find the old man smiling at me, revealing a wide space in his mouth where two or three upper teeth were missing. His clothes were old and worn, with thin patches here and there where the fabric had almost worn through and his shoes were

196

scuffed and lopsided as one side of each heel was worn down more than the other. His eyes, however, were bright, kind and interested and I felt friendly toward him right away. He said he couldn't help but overhear that I had a daughter.

"Oh," I said, surprised. "Yes... her name is Jill."

I knew I hadn't been talking about Jill, only thinking of her. Had Bruce or Chris mentioned her? I didn't think so; they were talking about the navy.

"Boy, I remember what it's like having a teenager in the house," the man said, grinning widely. I nodded sympathetically.

"They can be a handful," I said, wondering how he knew my daughter was a teenager.

"Yessiree," he agreed. "You know, my oldest son got into his share of scrapes but he never caused me all that much trouble, really. He went on to rank in the top of his class out there at Harvard. Now, he's enjoying raging success as the CEO of a hospital."

"Wow," I said, taken aback. This man certainly didn't look like the kind of person who could afford to put a son through Harvard. He looked like he could barely afford clothes! And what about those teeth? He must be making it up, I thought.

"But my younger son," he went on, "now he was a different story. Got in trouble every time he turned around. I can't tell you how many times I had to bail him out of jail for this petty thing or that. Stealing cars, driving drunk... he put me through it, let me tell you. Got so as I didn't even want to answer the phone when he called. But, you know, he grew out of it. He finally turned himself around and went on to school, graduated and everything; not at Harvard but you know it was a good school. And now he's a teacher - junior high. Doesn't make as much money as his brother but I would guess he's just as happy."

"Well, that's good," I said.

"But, you know, the funny thing," the man said, leaning toward me, "he told me some years ago that the reason why he got into so much trouble is because he was trying to get my attention. He felt swallowed up in the shadow of his successful brother, you know? He didn't think I loved him as much."

I stared at the funny little man next to me as he shook his head in regret.

"We're straightened out now," he said. "But, you know, we sure wasted a lot of time. A whole lot of trouble could have been avoided if I had just taken him into my arms and told him how much I loved him, and how proud of him I was."

"Oh..." I was at a loss for words.

"So, you just make sure you hug that daughter of yours," the old man told me. "You tell her how much you love her. It ain't easy being the second born. 'Specially when the older one is successful and good at getting attention; that's quite a shadow to be placed in."

I stared in disbelief at this man, who had now pushed his empty plate away from him and was getting up from the table. With a goodbye and a wave, he wobbled out of the restaurant on those crooked shoes and disappeared into the night. I turned to Chris and Bruce, demanding to know if they had heard anything.

"We aren't paying attention to you," Bruce teased.

"I just figured you were being nice to him," Chris said. "He looked really poor."

"And neither of you talked to him at all, or have ever seen him before?"

"No."

"Of course not, Mom."

I was really moved then, for I felt as though Spirit had spoken to me through that man since I was having such a hard time getting my messages in the usual way. How else could he have known so much about my children? How did he know that Chris was an older successful brother and that Jill was always complaining about not getting equal treatment? How did he even know Jill was the younger of the two? His advice was plain and simple, yet I knew it was exactly what I needed to hear.

Underneath all of her belligerent behavior, Jill was trying to get us to show her how much we truly loved her. She wasn't sure; for some reason she doubted that we did. Tears came to my eyes as I realized this and I thanked Spirit for reaching me through that scruffy old man. He was the perfect messenger because he was a paradox. His words didn't match his appearance, much as Jill's angry words disguised the true state of her mind. He seemed dirty and poor and unkempt, while describing his life as one of prosperity and love and, ultimately, success. Likewise, Jill had been coming across to me as a cruel and heartless brat, while really she was a beautiful, wise being still in the stages of development - a fact I had forgotten. I realized I had been caught up in the surface of things without delving into the truth underneath and this was why I found myself in such a state of confusion. Of course things would not make sense at the surface level because that didn't adequately reflect what was really going on. That was a mere distraction, just like the clothes and teeth of the old man.

Another time, a couple of years later, I walked into the school building where I worked, filled with anxiety about Chris. He was stationed down by Acapulco somewhere and had not called that weekend, even though he had said he would. I felt unnerved being out of touch with him for so long and couldn't help but worry about him. I felt that if I was worried, there must be something to it. Was I sensing something or just caught up in my own fears? It seemed impossible to tell for sure.

As I entered the building, a Vietnamese woman I knew only slightly came up to me and asked how my son was doing.

"He's fine," I answered, surprised. I had only spoken to this woman a couple of times and didn't think I had ever mentioned Chris to her but I assumed she had heard about his being in the navy through the grapevine.

"Where his boat?" she asked, in broken English. I told her he was stationed off the coast of Mexico down by Acapulco.

"Oh, my husband, me, we there too one time," she said, smiling excitedly, "it so warm, the sun so hot there! He have good time! He be happy there! You know, my husband brother in navy, he say it so good, it teach young people so much, it make them good, good people; it make person think *strong*! Not weak thoughts anymore, only strong."

She beamed at me as I smiled back and told her how great that was to hear.

"It's hard sometimes," I admitted, "having him so far away."

"Oh," she said, patting my arm, "whenever I start to worry, I think about my husband brother and what he say - I think no more weak thoughts - only strong!"

"You are an angel!" I blurted out, so thankful for her bubbling optimism. "I can't tell you how much I needed to hear words like that today."

"Well, I love you," she said, simply, and turned and walked away. I stared after her in astonishment, not knowing what to say. She didn't even know me and she was telling me she loved me? It had to be Spirit telling me that; I don't know if the woman was even aware that she'd said the words. Spirit knew what I needed to hear and also knew I wasn't getting it through the usual means, so again, I had been reached through another human being. I was so grateful! I floated through the rest of the day, thanking Spirit, so happy that Chris was okay and I had been doing all that useless worrying for nothing.

I am always on the lookout now, for people or animals to send me messages from spirit, and it happens all the time. There are no accidents, in my view. If I bump into someone at the supermarket, I pay attention. If someone drives in front of me, cutting me off, I pay attention. If the mailman is someone I have never seen before and says something that sparks a particular chord with me, I pay attention. The messages and hints and clues and miracles are around us every day, all the time! Spirit is relentless and steadfast in its guidance of us. Those in our Spirit Circles are watching and keeping track, knowing when we need help, knowing exactly what we need to hear or see or feel. All we have to do is ask, and then pay attention!

Grandmother Olga was not the kind of grandmother you read about in children's storybooks. She had her very own sense of rightness and vision, and no one ever dared to question her too far. She seldom opened up her mind or heart to anything that did not come from her very own set of rules and from the many responsibilities she assigned to herself. Most of her time and effort centered on her eight children and her kind, but often-unappreciated husband, John Nordin.

Big John Nordin did everything he could think of to please his beautiful but often critical wife Olga. She was tough and old-fashioned, would tolerate no nonsense and was extremely religious. Everything in her life was dedicated to God and the Church. She was a good Christian, fervent in her beliefs and a righteous, upstanding woman. No one had better tell her different, either, because Olga would upbraid that unlucky soul up one side and down the other! There was nobody brave enough to mention the words 'psychic' or 'ESP' around Grandma Olga, but we were all aware of her many visions that seemed to foretell the future. She attributed these visions to the power of God and to her own righteous behavior but I suspect she had inherited this ability through a long line of psychic oriented people.

One of these visions kept her and Grandpa John embroiled in a nasty argument that lasted two days until they finally realized what had happened.

Grandpa John had been driving the car, trying to be extra careful as he always was when Grandma Olga was in the passenger's seat, since she never did trust his driving abilities. They left their spacious country home to travel the back roads into Brainerd a few miles away, the engine working hard in the intense August heat. Across the flat countryside they went, much too slowly in John's opinion, much too fast in Olga's. Then, suddenly John found himself hitting the brakes as Olga screamed at him to stop.

"You almost ran him over, you fool!" she yelled at the top of her lungs. John slid into a noisy stop in the gravel alongside the road and turned to look behind him in alarm.

"He's injured," Olga screeched, hitting his arm, "get out there and help him!"

But John could see nobody in the road. In fact, there was no sign of another human as far as the eye could see!

"There isn't anyone there," he said to Olga. She craned her neck around and then got out of the car to look behind the back bumper. When she got back into the passenger seat, she was cursing at her husband in Swedish.

"I told you," he said, shaking his head.

"He was there," she insisted, "and you almost killed him with your careless driving."

John looked this way and that across the open plains. Anybody limping away, or even running at top speed, would still be in sight. There was no one around.

They argued all the way to town: Olga was sure she had seen someone lying injured in the road and John was just as sure she had not. They argued all the way back home later that afternoon and all through dinner. The next day they argued again. John knew he wasn't going to change her mind so he tried to let the matter rest but she kept bringing it up again, insistent that he admit she had seen someone.

Finally, two days after the incident, Olga and John heard from a friend that a neighbor man had been killed on that very stretch of highway just that morning, having been struck by a careless driver speeding toward town.

"I told you," Olga said to John, wagging a finger at him, "I saw that man lying there. You could have been the one to kill him, the way you drive."

Life with visions was very normal to Grandma Olga. She never once imagined that she possessed some type of psychic gift to which others would love to have access. To her mind, the visions were just another part of living a godly life. I don't know that they ever did her any good or helped her grow in any way - she treated them as matter-of-factly as she did anything else.

Likewise, my mother experienced strange phenomena in her life without thinking much of it and, except for telling the tales with some relish from time to time, she didn't really pursue these experiences with a yearning for insight and understanding. We children often heard about these things, such as the time she was suffering from pneumonia and a kindly nun came to sit with her while her parents and siblings went to the lake. This lovely nun cared for her with such love and tenderness that my mother was feeling almost completely better by the time the day was over. The nun was gone by the time the others got home but Vivian thanked Grandmother Olga profusely for sending someone to look after her while they were gone.

"She was so very nice," she said, gratefully.

"What," Olga replied, puzzled, "I didn't send anyone here to look after you."

"But the nun -"

"What nun?"

So, Vivian realized the nun had come from somewhere or someone else, although she never found out who, and never saw that nun again. But she knew what she knew and was always comforted by that memory when a kindly woman in black had come and cared for her so lovingly that lonely day.

Years later, I was to often wonder about this as I thought of people, so many people, who go through their entire lives without recognizing or caring much about the way Spirit touches their lives. Yet this did not seem to stop Spirit from intervening from time to time and making a significant impact. It made me curious as to how often and how much Spirit affects the lives of people, even when they are not looking for such assistance.

Partly because I wasn't sure about the answer to this question, and partly because I remembered so clearly how much of a misfit I felt like as a child, I raised my own children to look for the spiritual influences in their lives from the very beginning. I taught them to heed their own feelings and believe in their own visions. There was no such label as 'imaginary friend' in our house! I don't know if this is why they experienced so many things associated with the spiritual realm from very young ages, or if they were just naturally inclined this way because of something that seemed to run through their genes, but both of them had very clear experiences early on which were definitely connected to spirit.

Ever since Chris could talk, he was telling about the Green Man who always followed him around. During those early years he was so nonchalant about it he would forget to mention it unless the Green Man did something funny or out of the ordinary but whenever I would ask him where the Green Man was, he would look around and point.

"He's right there in the corner," he would say or, "He's up on the ceiling being goofy."

When he got to be a teenager, he kept the Green Man a secret from his friends most of the time but he never denied his presence and would still mention him to me from time to time. I came to count on that Green Man to look after my son and take care of him during those times when he became wild through his teen years, doing devilish acts and engaging in reckless behavior. Skydiving, racing, riding, driving: he did it all, and if I hadn't had faith in his spirit guides I would have been a nervous wreck *all* the time - even more than I was!

I've come to believe over the years that everyone is affected by spirit guidance each and every day of their lives. Many times they ignore the signs that are there but often people are steered this way or that without ever knowing they were not in the driver's seat at the time. I don't think there is such a thing as an ordinary life. I think all of life - *everyone's* life - is a miracle in motion.

Chris used to see beings from other dimensions from time to time when he was younger but now he sees countless numbers of them all the time. He can shift his eyes, usually at will, and tune into the sight of an entirely different dimension that overlays this one, and can see all kinds of beings doing all kinds of things. He says many of them do not seem aware of our dimension at all, even though they are so close. This is the way it is with us too, I am sure. If we could only shift our vision a little more often, we would be astounded at what we see.

There is magic around us at every turn, miracles going on all the time. Our very existence here on this planet is a miracle. The fact that millions of people drive down the freeways at seventy or eighty miles an hour to get to work every day and get to work on time without killing one another, is a miracle. Breathing is a miracle. So is a beating heart. So, we shouldn't feel so surprised at the miraculous nature of spirit working in our lives. We shouldn't be so skeptical about the influence of past lives or other dimensions - don't we see that our very life here is a miracle in progress?

One of the wonders of the human experience is the miracle of family. Whoever we chose to come here with, participating in a mutual drama is a very important part of our spiritual growth whether we like these people or not. Nobody influences us so much, especially in our early years, as our families. I have found it very therapeutic and enlightening to gather various stories of my family members, looking them over and discovering the various patterns and lessons within them. Part of accepting who we are is in the acknowledging and acceptance of where and who we came from because these have, in part, shaped the way we look at the world.

In my family, there has been a pattern of interest in psychic behavior, even though this was often suppressed or talked about under a different title, as with Grandma Olga. My sister Marlene has also had many visions and premonition dreams, although many of them are frightening to her as they were to me during childhood. Gary, our brother, also talked about psychic phenomena often while we were growing up, closely observing the many mysteries of the world and he had a keen interest in the powers of the mind. I remember him talking excitedly about what a different world one would see from the perspective of a blade of grass and, although many of our friends dismissed him as weird, his ramblings served to pique my own curiosity about such things.

A very important event concerning my brother Michael happened in 1980 when our father had been hospitalized in order to receive a blood transfusion. He was battling cancer and in need of new blood, although the doctors were quick to tell us the situation was not terribly serious at the moment. Just a routine treatment, they said.

I stood in the hospital corridor, waiting for Michael to show up so I could direct him to the open lounge down the hall where our father was resting with some other family members and watching television. Feeling rather optimistic, I hummed to myself as I waited, glad things were going so well with the transfusion, knowing my father would be feeling much better by the end of the day.

"Okay," Michael said, startling me out of a daydream. I smiled.

"Didn't hear you come up!"

I waved my hand in the direction of the family lounge where our father had gone to rest after his ordeal.

"This way," I said.

We began to walk down the brightly lit hall when suddenly Michael stopped dead in his tracks in front of room 518. He stared into the room in dismay, his face crumbling.

"What is it?" I cried, alarmed by the tears streaming down my brother's face. He collapsed against me, sobbing.

"Oh my god," he said, choking on his tears. "I didn't know he was dying!"

"What?"

I looked past him at the skinny old man lying in the bed there in room 518 who did, indeed, look as though he were

206

dying. But that old man couldn't have weighed more than 80 pounds, he was so shriveled up. How could Michael have mistaken him for our robust, 190-pound father who was sitting in the family lounge at that very moment, puffing on a cigar? But Michael was sure it was our father in that room, lying in that bed in room 518, dying right in front of us at that very moment. It took me quite some time to calm him down long enough to follow me down the hall to where our father really was, and even then he could not get that image out of his mind. He went back to that room, not believing he was wrong until he saw for himself that the dying old man was someone else.

We had no way of knowing it at the time but the blood transfusion our father received that day infected him with the AIDS virus. He suffered greatly as his health quickly declined and two years later he died at that same hospital. He had changed so drastically we could hardly recognize him as the man we had known all our lives. He couldn't have weighed more than 80 pounds. And the room he died in... was room 518. The very room where Michael had seen the vision of him two years before.

This experience and others have caused Michael to avoid any type of future knowledge like the plague. He does not want to see what he cannot change or understand. Premonitions are fearful to him, as they were to me once, and so he blocks them out as best he can although sometimes information will seep through anyway, much to his distress.

When I look around at family members, I see so many things they have taught me just through being who they are and going through their own life dramas. Our sister Pam was the nurturing one, teaching me the power of caring and gentleness even during frightening times. Terry and Michael are artists, revealing the power of capturing beauty on paper; Mark is a writer with a very unique way of looking at the world around him, always able to show me a different viewpoint; while Tor, the oldest of us, demonstrated the path of detachment as he moved far away and kept to himself. Family has forced me to learn about boundaries, learning when and how to say 'no' or to turn away from someone I love. I have also learned patience and acceptance, knowing I cannot change the path of another if they are not willing participants in such a change. I have watched the effects of substance abuse as it robs those I love of their power and ability and I have seen the sadness of those who are not in touch with their own inner beings, watching the light in their eyes grow dimmer and dimmer over the years as they numb themselves to who they really are.

All these things have taught me so much. I am grateful for sobriety and for being able and willing to live a spiritual life. I am grateful, as well, for the many wonderful traits of family that shine through in spite of the troubles. I have been led to ask many questions of Spirit because of the way my family is and was, and have learned much because of this. I have learned that those who choose to live their lives in misery are also serving others because they are providing insights and lessons at many levels that will be used for all time. They are also affecting many of us at the human level as we hold our own lives in comparison and learn about gratitude and compassion.

One can never tell where messages and gifts will come to us from the spirit realm. Often they come in the form of a stranger's remark or an odd coincidence or by some other unexpected avenue. We will be more likely to pick up on these many treasures if we have our eyes open and are paying close attention to what is going on around us. Sometimes, a profound insight will come through an experience that seems very negative to us at the outset and it is only later that we see what a blessing it was. When one has an ever-deepening trust in Spirit, these gifts and nuggets of knowledge become more easily apparent and show up in a person's life more often. Look around with the keen eyesight of a hawk; you don't want to miss what Spirit has in store for you!

Love has a flowering
statement - a music
all its own - swaying
in a gentle breeze the
sky tames an angry sun
washes over a rain smell
and from underneath all of
this, the world rising up
with one small bird
flying through the air.

Michelle Senjem and Rebecca LeTourneau

Conscious Connections

I am continually amazed when I wake up in the morning and look around me, for I see miracles everywhere. Spirit dances across our world with great joy and glee, rearranging, shifting, molding, startling, soothing - always interacting with us on a great many levels. I never know what is going to happen when I walk out the door, who I am going to bump into, what I am going to hear or see. I do know that Spirit is involved, though, and knowing this keeps me in a continual state of awe and anticipation, for whatever is coming, I know I have agreed to it and have had a hand in planning it! I know this is true because I have met and recognized the part of me that is spirit, the authentic soul of my Spirit Circle Self, so I am aware that there are many dimensions to this person I call "Me" and that I will hopefully recognize the clues which are set out to capture my attention. Of course, sometimes I miss things. But I have seen enough and have experienced enough to know the importance of looking for miracles, because I know I will miss so much more if I don't!

Many of us believe in a spirit world and will profess some kind of faith in miracles and/or divine guidance. But how many of us feel a strong conscious connection to spirit? How many of us have had illumination experiences that enable us to know without a doubt that the spirit world is very real and is a very close part of our existence?

I would say a good many of us do feel this connection and have had illumination experiences of some kind that served to reinforce a trust in spirit. Most people, when asked, will recount some strange incident from childhood perhaps, or from their adult life when they encountered some form of spirit, or when a bizarre event served to prove the presence of spirit in the person's mind. This shows how strongly connected we really are to our roots: even those who are not interested in things of a spiritual nature can usually recall something in their lives that caused them to believe there is more to human life than meets the eye.

Every human culture across the globe in every time frame of history has felt moved to define its connection to spirit. The need to understand and acknowledge this connection seems inherent within the human species. Even those who claim to have no belief in a spirit realm are often motivated to replace this notion with one of scientific mystery, such as a big bang theory which really holds no more convincing proof within it than any supernatural belief does. What is truly interesting these days is the progression of science toward spiritual understanding. More and more logical-minded people are beginning to recognize the divine mysterious and spiritual nature of science itself - of the entire physical world.

Yet, even as we hold beliefs in some form or another of life after death and God and spirit life, how much do we really feel a part of these things every day? How strongly connected do we feel to it all?

I believe it is possible to live very close to bliss nearly every day - even while still in human form. Sure, there will be problems and surprises and even heartbreak but a solid understanding and recognition of one's connection to spirit will make even the worst bumps in life's road go more smoothly. If there is something within us that is anchored to Absolute Knowing, we can be shaken from our center now and then but will spring right back to it in no time, for anything else will quickly become unsavory, feeling foreign and uncomfortable. Once you have been well grounded in a sincere understanding of Spirit and of the reality of who you are, you cannot forget it. No matter what happens after that, you know the difference between life lived from the center and life lived from the confused edges of awareness.

I could, for example, decide to ignore and reject all I have learned over the years. I could wake up tomorrow and tell myself none of it happened, it is all hooey and I am going to avoid anything having to do with spirit work in the future. I could tell myself this but deep inside my being there is a *knowing* that cannot be rooted out no matter what I say or do. Without a doubt I would find myself drawing on Ging's courage and fierce strength if some frightening event caught me off guard. Whenever I felt moved to nurse an animal or plant back to good health, I would feel the compassionate interest of Marcus swirling through me. Each time I found myself hesitating about something I really wanted to do, I would feel Maricell's desperate longing for freedom. And, most of all, I would catch myself time and time again seeking Baji's help and gentle guidance when life began to confuse me too much. These are not things I can think away because the experiences I have had are too real and too profound and have impacted upon my consciousness too deeply.

Now, of course, I cannot even imagine trying to disengage myself from the wonders of Spirit that have shaped my life. But the point is, I know I *couldn't* even if I wanted to! This is how deeply the connection is felt and how powerful its influence is over my day-to-day existence. My conscious mind might try to deny the experiences I have had and the emotions I have felt in accordance with these experiences but my unconscious mind - along with all the other dimensions of my being - would know better and would not be fooled. Truth is, I doubt very much that even my conscious mind could be fooled to such a degree.

Not everyone reaches this point of inner knowing at the same time or in the same way but all can reach it if they choose. All that is needed is a conscious intention and a dedication to strengthen the connection to Spirit that is already there, and to bring it more into the conscious realm of one's thinking.

When one becomes focused on reinforcing this invisible eternal bond, life begins to shift and change in a million subtle ways. Gradually, all of existence becomes a moving, dancing miracle in which one is participating. There is meaning to everything after a while, from the gently falling leaf to the hurricanes in the sea to the war-torn Middle East to the smell of cookies baking in the oven. A new sacredness seems to permeate everything as one begins to recognize the spiritual nature of every tiny particle making up this physical world.

The clarity of one's vision improves drastically as one begins to see things from a wider, more eternal perspective. There is no longer a need to get so caught up in much of the clutter and noise of the world, for the true interests of one's authentic nature will draw one's focus into a particular direction, concentrating creative energy where it can do the most good.

If you are seeking to strengthen your conscious bonds with spirit, make it a priority. Think about it. Start paying attention, especially to your own body, your own feelings, your own thoughts and desires and fears. Get to know the real you, the you that has always been hiding in there behind those eyes, under that skin, beneath that beating heart. Talk to yourself, talk to spirits you cannot see, listen for the whisperings of familiarity, which have long been hovering at the edges of your awareness. Somewhere deep inside you, know that you are much more than what the world sees, much more than you can communicate to others. Get in touch with this eternal wisdom within, pull it out, dust it off and study it intensely.

Also, pay heed to what draws your attention in the outer world. What catches your eye? What makes your heart leap with joy? What makes you laugh? What repels you? These are all clues to your inner nature - learn to recognize them. Become familiar with the patterns in your life and dissect them, delving inside them to find those hidden motivations.

Never take anything for granted. If you break a glass in the sink, stop and reflect on your thoughts and emotions. What is your energy like at that moment? What is your focus? What crosses your mind as you hold your bleeding finger under the faucet? While watching the evening news, which stories hold your interest? Why? When you first wake up in the morning,

how do you feel? What kinds of thoughts are running through
your mind? Question yourself continually as you begin to tune in
to who you are. Challenge any long-held assumptions you have
about yourself. Try a new perspective; imagine how you look
from various viewpoints you wouldn't normally hold. Realize
there are many parts of your nature you have not discovered yet!
Open yourself up to the possibilities and monitor your system as
you go. Prepare to be surprised, delighted, intrigued, awed, and
even a bit frightened at times as you discover more and more of
your nature, deeper levels of your being and the many new twists
and turns of your creative desires.

Another very effective way to bond with spirit in a conscious
way is through play and fun. We forget sometimes that laughter
and hilarity are spiritual gifts! There are many insights available
to us through the childlike aspects of our nature. Go sledding
down a big hill screaming your head off, taking careful note of
your emotions, thoughts and feelings the entire time. Splash
around in the water, roll around in the grass, jump up and down,
trying to touch the stars. We don't do ourselves any favors by
being so serious about things. And, if you are open to the idea,
many playful spirits will begin to drift into your conscious life.
They will play tricks on you, turning your radio on and off,
opening and shutting a window, moving things from where you
placed them just moments before. Listen closely for the giggling
that is no doubt going on as you search frantically for your keys
or your checkbook or that special charm you feel you just cannot
live without!

When my children were young, we often played games in
order to develop our psychic abilities. One of these games was
done in separate rooms, as each of us would draw an object on a
piece of paper, seeing if we could tune into the other's thoughts
and draw the same object. Other times we would try to come up
with the same color or number or letter. Often, we were exactly
right. Other times our drawings wouldn't match but even many

of these times would reflect some aspect of something one of us had been thinking about. It began to dawn on me that children are naturally very intuitive beings. Chris and Jill amazed me again and again with the insights they would pick up on without even trying.

The kids also participated with my friend Jana and I as we spent many hours with the Channel Box, gleaning messages from some faraway ancestors. Through much laughter and joking, we were somehow able to pick up on the meanings meant for us at the time and actually learned a great many lessons during our crazy fun. Even today, one of the kids will come and remind me of something going on in one of our lives now and say, "Remember the Channel Box told us this?" And we will sit and be amazed together, laughing at the way Spirit often surprises us.

One of these surprises came back to us when Chris was stationed outside of Washington State for a time, because when looking through some old notes I found some messages recorded from Channel Box play when Chris was only eight years old. In one particular session, it had said that Chris would be a man on a boat ... and when asked where, it said... WASHINGTON STATE. So, this was just one of those things that seems alarming at first until it is remembered that we are dealing with Spirit here so it shouldn't be surprising at all, while at the same time it is incredible and amazing.

Many profound messages and clues can come to us through play, and much spiritual development can take place, too. When I began to become interested in astral travel, I played around with energy quite a bit, making it a daily habit to raise my arm up out of its skin and watch the energy of my spirit self rise above the physical. I would sit somewhere for hours, while watching television with the family, or visiting with friends, and just keep lifting my spirit arm up and then letting it fall back down into the physical arm. It was so incredibly fun to play around with spirit this way! I practiced and practiced, all body parts bit by bit, until I was able to lift my entire body out at once and take to flight, leaving my physical body behind. This was made possible through play!

Baji: *It is true that many people go through life with blinders on, refusing at some level to see the miraculous nature of their existence. Yet, if the veil were totally lifted from the human mind, there would be no more need for the human experience! A bit of the veil is always needed so that the adventures within the earthly plane can serve their purpose.*

Still, a person can train his or her self to catch glimpses beyond the veil. The more you see of other worlds and dimensions, the more the veil falls away. Expanding one's vision can truly enhance and expand the quality of human life, for it strengthens the conscious connection to Spirit. But remember, there is no need to see everything all at once. It is better to relax and enjoy the human experience as it unfolds, gaining new insights bit by bit. Go ahead and have ordinary days. Let your mind rest, kick back and watch TV, visit with friends, go shopping, play games, chitchat about nonsense. This does not diminish the fact that you are a spiritual being at all. In fact, such frivolities help to keep you balanced while in human form, as long as you focus on aspects of Spirit as well. You are here to be human after all, and if your head is always in the clouds, you won't be able to see where your feet are planted.

Yes, miracles are happening every millisecond of every day, all around you. In fact, there are so many miracles going on, you can't really call them miracles by your definition. Indeed, what you would call miracles are really quite common occurrences - so I guess you could call them ordinary! But, from the human perspective, a miracle is a very surprising event which inspires awe, so one could still think of them as miracles, since one could be continually surprised and awed every day of his or her life.

Look at the sky, the grass, the trees... feel the wind on your face. Even these things that you witness every day should continually surprise you and fill you with awe. Your foot sways back and forth as you talk on the phone; you are not even aware of it but there it goes, back and forth, back and forth. Your brain is directing your happy foot even as your full concentration is on your friend's voice in your ear. This is a miracle! This is an astounding thing! Look out at the world differently, let yourself be amazed.

Once you begin to see the world in this new light, your thinking changes. You will begin to notice more and more amazing things. You will become more aware of the miraculous nature of your human experience, and this recognition sets you in a closer alignment with Spirit. Thus, your life takes on added dimensions. There is more meaning behind everything you experience; there is a new purpose to all that you do. You feel the difference intensely, for now you understand yourself as spirit and soul, as a part of something bigger and more divine than that which you can readily see.

Don't obsess, however. Even while recognizing you are spirit, remember you are also human, which means you have agreed to certain limitations for the time being. As you grow increasingly aware of the true nature of your surroundings, you will see the magic of your adventure without really trying so hard. It becomes a natural way of seeing the world. So, there is no need to force yourself into being a constant watchdog poised for awe at every second. Such an approach would be counterproductive anyway, since you would be merely imposing your will where it doesn't belong and would probably distract yourself quite a bit from where you really want to be.

Allow yourself to play and indulge in the earthly adventures that interest you. Much is learned by all you say and do, whether you are acting from a focused state or not. Just be alert so that when something does jump out at you, you will recognize it. Don't get so caught up in earthly pursuits that you lose your way and miss out on the magic. Balance is the key. You can enjoy while you learn and learn while you enjoy. You can see your ordinary life as one filled with miracles or not: it's up to you. Just know if you decide to blind yourself to the magic, you are really missing out!

Some suppose that one must be born with some strange and awesome "gift" in order to consider themselves psychic but this is not so. Life itself is a strange and awesome gift - one we have given ourselves, actually, and we are all participating in this human existence on a psychic level as well as a physical one. Just take some time to browse through a picture book of pregnancy and the process the fetus, as well as the mother, goes through! This is a curious and magical development and one we have all been through. Thus, we have been touched by the miraculous even before making our entrance into this physical world.

This magic, this miracle of life and nature, is all around us all the time. We are connected to it all, to everything and everyone, and there are many, many helps for us along our life journey. All we have to do is open our eyes and pay attention. Of course, most of us have been taught to trust only those things that we can 'prove' through our senses of sight, smell, hearing, taste, and touch. But how much do we really pay attention to even these things? How well do we listen to what our bodies are telling us? There is so much information that comes to us through these senses that is subtle and beyond our awareness. There is also much that we see that others do not and vice versa.

So, who is right? If someone is convinced she has seen an angel, how do we know that she has not? If a person claims he heard a voice thunder at him to jump out of the way just as a roaring motorcycle careened around a corner, even though there was no one else around, how can we say he is wrong? Much of the world is a mystery. Our very existence is a mystery. Being a part of this great mystery is shared by all, just as is the miracle of being alive.

Everyone has the choice as to how they are going to look at the world, at life. Life is a wonder, all we experience serves to shape our spirits, to form who we are and what we are becoming. This, too, is a miracle. Not all choose to acknowledge that what they are experiencing is a part of the magic, the mystery we all came from and are going to. Not all will see that they are divine and important and here on this earth for a profound purpose. But many others do see. Many already feel and know that they are venturing forth on a great adventure, impacting the world in a wonderfully unique way. These psychic adventures happen to all of us, no matter how insignificant and mundane our lives may seem. If we don't see it, then we are missing out on one of the most mind-boggling, exciting ingredients life has to offer.

Remember the joy of being alive. The great abundance and goodness that life, in all its ups and downs, has in store for us. We are only here on this planet for a short time; we should make the most of it and engage in our earth-lives wholeheartedly.

Authenticity is the key. No one has to make something up about himself or herself to be important; we are all treasures and we are all psychic. All we have to do is notice.

Here I sit
With the world around me
I am experiencing everything
From a chilling breeze
To my own soft skin

Michelle Senjem and Rebecca LeTourneau

A Message From Baji:

I hope to inspire all to feel love and compassion - first for themselves and then for others. Things we focus on EMERGE, so... focus with care.

It is a truth to say I am Michelle, in a way. I am an energy that shifts and changes for her needs and I have appeared in many forms and with many voices - sometimes to amuse as well as to guide. My intense interest and love for Michelle is that of a parent, for this is my primary role with her now - her being my creation, a manifestation of my own creative talents developed over many, many lifetimes. You see, each person on earth is a part of a larger system; the soul is not solitary, there are many dimensions to it. I am a part of Michelle's 'system' - we are of the same soul, along with others. Each of you has this same group entity aspect to your soul and each one in the group is there to assist and guide and love YOU, for you are the physical manifestation this time around, you are the one who dove into the earth realm and volunteered to take on this human role for the period of a physical lifetime.

I am here to encourage and inspire Michelle to be joyful, which is the purpose of this book, but also to spread this joy and hope around, which is the obvious effect of one's joyful creativity. In Michelle's yearning to know absolutely EVERYTHING (!), she has traveled many roads and has influenced many people, which is as it should be. She is here this time around to learn and to teach, to share and to gather information for all of us. This is where her interest lies and what brings her the most joy, so this is where I also direct my energies today.

Everyone has a multidimensional spirit but not every human will want to know this right now, which is also as it should be, for they have come here to be simply human and are satisfied with that. Let it be. For others, the pull from the spiritual dimension is so strong they feel compelled to embark upon a spiritual exploration, which is also something they had planned for this earthly adventure. Get to know yourself honestly, and then go where your interests lead you.

Trust life.

You have the wisdom of many worlds within you and there is much more to YOU than you know. So there is no need to feel alone. There is no need to be frightened and hesitant about life, about experience, about going forward. Don't you know that the WHOLE of you will take care of the human PART of you? Trust in your soul, in all its dimensions, for you are its ultimate concern. And, as each soul grows and learns and expands its awareness, it touches the souls of others, and on and on, and with this the whole universe changes every second, every millisecond for all time.

Onward we go, creating, loving, learning, laughing, trying new things, discovering new avenues of expression, revealing more and more of who and what we are, which is DIVINE. Think of God and then you get the idea; we are all a part of that eternal entity which many think of as God, yet we are manifested in parts, so that the whole can continue. Creating, creating, creating: this is our interest, this is our reason for being, with the goal of Absolute Joy and Love always behind our explorations.

Evil is not as complex as many would make it out to be; it is simply the ignorance of the potential for love and compassion which every soul contains. There are many worlds and many lives in existence this very moment and the dark side is a part of this, too. It is a necessary part of the explorations that lead us forward, because without it there would be no joy, no love, no happiness. Misery and fear and other negative things constitute the mirror we must face if we are to fully cross the bridge to love and joy. Some spirits are immersed in this dark side as well as many humans but this is not a permanent state. This is but a step in the process, a murky puddle in the path to creative endeavors, and an illusory one at that. Do not dwell in these places any longer than is necessary; there is much help at your disposal to pull yourself out of it.

Pray. Direct your energy to what brings you joy.

Reach out and pull goodness to you with all the urgency of life, for this is what will make you sing. This is what will move you toward the bliss you seek. Yes, the negative is there, but there is always the other side. You will choose which side to turn your attention to. You will choose where to focus your eyes. You will choose which direction to follow. The choice is the magic.

The choice is a divine gift of life. Use it well.

Michelle Senjem and Rebecca LeTourneau

Who we are

We are sometimes lost
sometimes not ourselves,
we give up
or go on
some light will always escape.

The moon becomes a star
and the star
a million years from us.

Michelle Senjem and Rebecca LeTourneau

About the Authors

Michelle Senjem has been a practicing clairvoyant and psychic reader for more than twenty years. In addition to this work, she has also been employed in other helping fields involving the St. Paul public school system and the Hazeldon Drug Treatment Center. She has held workshops and public readings in Minnesota and continues to offer private readings by appointment. Her past work includes a weekly column in *The Edge* newspaper called *Ask Mija* and various articles and poetry published in the *Laki Lines*, Literary Ezine. She is co-founder of Mystic Waves, Inc., which includes a spiritual retreat online at mysticwaves.com. This is her first full-length book.

Rebecca LeTourneau, B.A. is co-founder of the *Laki Lines* Ezine and has published various short stories as in *Wood Framed Eagle* which was originally published *in A Room of One's Own*, vol.20:4, Winter 1997/98. Co-founder of Mystic Waves, Inc., she is currently working on a novel while continuing her work in graphic arts and web design. This is her first full-length book.

*Michelle Senjem and Rebecca LeTourneau have also written *Warrior Ghosts*, the first in *The Green Man Series*. A metaphysical novel, *Warrior Ghosts* depicts the struggles of young males in the inner city who receive guidance from a most unlikely character. The second novel in this series is *Mirror Lake*, the story of identical twins who experience tragic separation when one falls into a coma after a terrible accident. The only connection they have is through the dreamscape, a land both authors know well.

Printed in the United States
4464

9 780759 670617